PRAISE FOR RUN LIKE A PIRATE

"It's so easy to make an excuse as to why we can't eat right or work out . . . until you read *Run Like a Pirate*! This is the tush kicking you need to make your goals happen and to know that you have a choice in taking care of yourself—physically and emotionally. What will your choice be? Start here!"

—**LaVonna Roth**, creator and founder of Ignite Your S.H.I.N.E.®

"There's something special about a person who has dedicated their life to improving the lives of others. Adam's *Run Like a Pirate* rem̲   ̲hat we have all we need inside to reach whatever ̲   b; we just have to focus on some of the   ace."

—**Steve Mesler**, Olympic gold ̲   ̲ons

"Are you going through the moti̲   ̲stuck? Tired of making excuses for why yc   ̲plished this or that? Adam's authentic storytelling style i̲ ̲un *Like a Pirate* will draw you in and motivate you to try something hard. Your mindset will shift, and you will not only begin the race, you will also challenge yourself to reach seemingly unattainable goals. Don't wait. Start today."

—**Tara Martin**, author of *Be REAL*

"Adam is 100 percent inspiration, and so is this book. The upper-limit challenges we place on ourselves don't have to be there, and this book will show you how to accomplish any major goal that has slipped through your hands—until now."

—**Danny "Sunshine" Bauer**, host of the *Better Leaders Better Schools* podcast

"*Run Like a Pirate* is a master class in motivation, mindset, and mental/ physical endurance for educators and fitness enthusiasts alike. Author Adam Welcome's insightful journey from runner to elite marathoner gives readers the roadmap for success in the classroom and on the bumpy trails of life as we travel the path of health and wellness. This is a must-read for anyone who loves education, physical fitness, or phenomenal storytelling. Go get this book today. Hurry. Run!"

—**Weston Kieschnick**, bestselling author of *Bold School*, senior fellow, International Center for Leadership in Education

"This book is a celebration of life priorities as much as it is a story of inspiration or accomplishment. Adam's story and twelve-month challenge are simply a vehicle for celebrating his commitment to helping others achieve their dreams. Loaded with simple mantras like 'Just. Start.' and 'You gotta chill,' this book is one part personal trainer, one part life coach, and all parts cheering section. He's in it . . . for us to win it! Outstanding. I'm proud to call him a friend!"

—**Basho Mosko**, creator of BASHO & FRIENDS, partner at FuelEd Schools

"*Run Like a Pirate* is an uplifting, inspiring, and empowering book not only about long distance running but also—as the subtitle suggests—pushing ourselves in whatever we do to get more out of life. Adam Welcome's humble approach to sharing the story of his prodigious accomplishments is one that will resonate with anyone interested in performing at high levels. This is a book that will keep you turning the pages and cheering along every step of the journey."

—**Jeffrey Zoul**, EdD, author, speaker, leadership coach, and president of ConnectEDD

"In *Run Like a Pirate*, Adam inspires us all not only to live a better life but to be passionate about our work! As a runner and principal myself, I understand the sacrifices that he makes to be a blesser and not a stressor to his colleagues and students. This book is a must-read if you plan to change your life and the lives of others!"

—**Salome Thomas-El**, award-winning principal, speaker, and author

"*Run Like a Pirate* resonated deeply on many levels, as I drew many parallels to my journey as an educator. Adam beautifully illustrates the power of setting giant goals and not letting anything stand in the way of achieving them. This book will inspire, empower, challenge, and encourage you to live a life full of passion. No excuses!"

—**Tisha Richmond**, tech instructional coach and author of *Make Learning Magical*

"Adam's message of continuing to push forward and enjoying the journey along the way will always stick with me. I believe I will be referencing *Run Like a Pirate* in my life a lot, especially when excuses start to come to mind. After reading Adam's book, I'm so inspired to set all of my excuses aside and start a #RunStreak. Thank you for inspiring me and many others, Adam!"

—**Akram Osman**, associate principal

"*Run Like a Pirate* makes me want to get out there and do more. What excuses? What insecurities? What perceived roadblocks? You've got time, you've got the wherewithal, you've got one life, and according to Adam, your bandwidth is far wider than you could possibly fathom. Take these words and apply them to your deepest dreams. *Run Like a Pirate* should be the handbook for anyone who dares to believe that there's more to life than simply living. Go do great, hard things!"

—**Kim Van Acker**, educator and marathoner,
Hyland's 2018 All-Teacher Team

"Although I would still call Adam 'crazy,' I realize people say the same thing about my marathon running/training with students. Adam's book is a validation of the marathon running community and an inspiration to continue to get the most out of life."

—**Rachel Rodriguez**, mother, runner, teacher, coach

"*Run Like a Pirate* is a book about constantly pushing yourself and taking on life's challenges with a positive attitude. Though the title may suggest this is all about running, it is so much more, as it is a motivating and inspirational read. Many amazing contributors are embedded throughout the book, and the short chapters make it easy to read. Adam's passion and energy for life come through in this book, and I found myself reading the entire book in one weekend. I highly recommend reading this book and joining Adam's energy and passion for life."

—**Jonathan Eagan**, assistant superintendent

"We are made for so much more than we allow ourselves to experience, and that is a thread throughout Adam Welcome's *Run Like a Pirate*. Adam's book was the kick I needed to genuinely challenge myself again as a classroom teacher, mother, and runner. I dare you to try and not want to run a marathon, ride a century, climb a mountain, whatever your thing might be after reading—actually, more like while reading. I hadn't even finished reading before I pulled out the calendar to start planning to run another marathon."

—**Ash Hickey**, mom, teacher, runner, dreamer of big dreams

"Adam Welcome dares all of us to actions that enable us to become the best version of ourselves. His words illustrate the importance of dreaming big, cultivating positivity, and embracing opportunities to impact yourself and others. A must-read for anyone looking to be inspired!"

—**Becky Ince**, principal, curriculum director, lead learner, and runner

"Whether you are a runner, want to be a runner, or just want to be inspired for life, *Run Like a Pirate* is the book for you. *Run Like a Pirate* is filled with stories through Adam's incredible running journey along with lessons that apply to any passion (not just running). *Run Like a Pirate* will motivate you to get up and go chase your own dreams, right now!"

—**Jessica Johnson**, principal, author, and speaker

"*Run Like a Pirate* is not just about running; it's about life. It's a tool to help you learn how to find your passion, immerse yourself into what you love, determine the people who support you, learn what it takes to get you there, transform your habits to achieve what's perceived by others as impossible, and—most importantly—achieve all of this with a positive mindset that will transform and inspire those around you."

—**Lori Connely-Vanderborne**, fitness-focused mother, educational leader, and change agent

"This book speaks to anyone who is looking for inspiration to 'go make it happen.' Filled with stories, tips, and motivation, Adam's book will bring you laughter and tears and will fill you with a desire to build a dream, make a plan, and find your 'crew.'"

—**Amber Heffner**, executive director of Illinois Computing Educators

"*Run Like a Pirate* by Adam Welcome is an inspiring book filled with relatable anecdotes for running enthusiasts from all walks of life that is motivating while also being raw about things not always going his way. This book will make you want to lace up your shoes and get moving before life passes you by."

—**Kelsey Godfrey**, teacher and running podcast host

"Years ago, I became so caught up in the hype and noise of running that I forgot why I ever started running in the first place. Now, as a busy classroom teacher, speaker, and author myself, I'm inspired by Adam to run 'Barney Style (as in Barney Rubble).' Not barefoot like Barney, but more simply, to just get out there and run. I'm taking Adam's advice and ditching all the noise. I'm going to run for myself, not for a time. I'm going to run to just experience life, my best life. Now, off I go—just me, my shoes, and the open road!"

—**Christina Nosek**, classroom teacher, author, and speaker

RUN
Like a
PIRATE

PUSH YOURSELF
TO GET MORE OUT OF LIFE

Adam Welcome

Run Like a PIRATE
© 2018 by Adam Welcome

Published by Dave Burgess Consulting, Inc.
San Diego, CA
DaveBurgessConsulting.com

Cover Design by Genesis Kohler
Editing and Interior Design by My Writers' Connection
Author Photos by Sarah Anne Bettelheim of Sarah Anne Photography

Library of Congress Control Number: 2018949409
Paperback ISBN: 978-1-946444-91-2
Ebook ISBN: 978-1-946444-93-6

First Printing: July 2018

DEDICATION

This book is dedicated to everyone who never had anyone in their corner cheering them on and telling them they can go farther and dig deeper—telling them to believe in themselves. This book is for you because I believe you can and you will.

CONTENTS

FOREWORD

BY HAMISH BREWER, AKA THE RELENTLESS PRINCIPAL

People often fall into three simple categories: those who let life pass them by, those who talk about doing something, and those who actually go out and live life to the fullest—regardless of the result.

Run Like a Pirate isn't just about Adam Welcome's quest to run in and complete marathons. It's about developing the right mindset, seizing the opportunity, and enjoying the journey!

Life is an opportunity, and once you believe you *are* something and can *be* someone, you can achieve anything! Being successful in life is about holding yourself accountable and believing you can accomplish something special when you put your heart and mind to it.

Run Like a Pirate is a challenge to us all. What are we doing when no one's watching, when no one is patting us on the back and telling us how awesome we are? Do we have the courage and conviction to do what we said we would do and be who we said we would be? Adam asks, "Why not?"

Life is not going to give you a handout; you have to go make things happen. The world we live in is a tough and unforgiving place that can swallow you up if you allow it. If you listen to the naysayers and allow negativity to set in, you will not accomplish anything—and probably not start anything.

This book shows us that life will provide every opportunity for success, if we put ourselves in a position to succeed with the right process and mindset. Life is about living, failing, and succeeding. When you share Adam's relentless PIRATE mindset, you begin to live life to the fullest and cross the finish line as a winner.

Everyone's journey in accomplishing a goal is different. We are all in different places with various levels of ability, time, and skill. What isn't different is the opportunity to start.

I've lived my life with a chip on my shoulder—with the mindset that whether I win or lose, I will make every effort to prove the world wrong. I am relentless in my pursuit of excellence for myself—and excellence for kids. Sometimes life is about taking chances and becoming a maverick to tackle challenges and opportunities head on.

Run Like a Pirate is a challenge to live beyond the limits of popular expectations—and an inspiration to stand up and be relentless.

As Adam says, it's time to push yourself to get more out of life!

WARMING UP

I've been an athlete my entire life. I've been what I would call a "casual runner" for years. I ran hard when I needed to and trained on a weekly basis, but it pretty much ended there. Until, I decided to run—like a pirate.

I've also spent my life searching for more, for the next challenge, for bigger, better, and harder. So the *Run Like a Pirate* mindset developed naturally for me. This approach to life is a commitment to doing what needs to be done in order to achieve more than ever before.

In the following pages, I'll share my running journey with you. You'll read about some of my friends—educators across the United States—who share my passion for running. By sharing the lessons we've learned (and are continuing to learn), my hope is that you'll be inspired to strive for more. This book focuses on running, but the message is about more than marathons; it's about giving your best—your all. Whatever you do in life, do it with the PIRATE attitude.

Passion

Pirate leaders bring their passion to work. They also work to identify and bring out the passions of their staff members and students.

Immersion

Remember that you only have one life; give it all you have, every single day.

Rapport

The people around you in life are needed for those tough times; build those relationships and rapport for when the going gets tough.

Ask and Analyze

How can I get there, and what's it going to take? Challenge and success are not for the faint of heart, but nothing worth having in life is.

Transformation

When you want something bad enough, and you set the goals high enough, you're bound to transform into something you've never been before.

Enthusiasm

With all the enthusiasm you can muster, go for it!

People have been questioning my ideas and goals my entire life. Heck, even my wife rolled her eyes when I told her about my running goals for 2017, and she's my biggest fan and partner in adventure. I've never worried about what other people think or say—or the laughs or smirks or doubt they may throw at me.

My ideas and goals aren't extreme, dangerous, or crazy. I just view life through a different lens than most. I want to realize my full potential as a human, and I try to squeeze every last drop of energy from my body. When I'm done, I walk away—and move on to what's next with no regrets.

Run Like a Pirate is a lifestyle—a mindset that compels me to give 100 percent to whatever activity I pursue. For me, that activity in 2017 was running. There's just nothing like it. The pain of a long race, the thoughts in your brain, the camaraderie with other runners, and the discipline of daily training despite cold weather, rain, darkness, and fatigue—that's the work nobody sees. But all of those challenges build on one another and are vital to crossing the finish line.

Not everybody is a runner, of course. You might hike, walk, swim, bike, do jazzercise, crossfit, or yoga. Maybe you have a passion that doesn't involve physical exercise at all. Pushing yourself is about what you *can* do, what you *want* to do, and what you think you *can't* do. The payoff comes when you achieve the goal. That's what life is all about. That's what running like a pirate is all about. That's how you get results.

I want you to experience the payoff.

That's why I'm going to ask you to do something challenging. And I promise, the payoff will be worth your effort.

In December of 2016, I decided to add more intensity in my life. After running a 3:36 marathon (twenty-six and two-tenths of a mile in three hours and thirty-six minutes) at the California International Marathon, I decided it was time for something big, new, and different.

This *something* had to be feasible and fit into my life as a husband, father, educator, author, and speaker. But more than that, I wanted to look inside my mind and sift through all the clutter. What I really wanted to do was increase the level of intensity in my life, to see what I really had inside.

Eureka! I'll run one marathon every month in 2017! I already knew the amazing feeling that came with crossing the finish line after taking thousands of little steps. I knew the mental and physical effort it took to complete a marathon. But I wondered, *Could I keep the focus and discipline for 365 days while working full time, being a father, a husband, and everything else?*

In all honesty, running monthly marathons wasn't an idea that had been brewing in the clutter of my mind. I had put some thought into running a few ultras the coming year, but when that thought popped into my head one morning—halfway through a ten-mile run—I knew I was going to make it happen.

That's kind of been a pattern throughout my life. An idea sprouts, and I go for it—no waiting, no excuses, just go!

Running twelve marathons, training for them, recovering from them, eating all those calories—that would be my sieve for the clutter and a path to clarity. When you push your limits of pain, month after month, day after day, you're forced to hone in on what's really important. Your brain can only process so many ideas and thoughts at once, running would help to sift through it all. And the pain would be an added bonus.

The wheels immediately started to spin in my brain: *Can I even run twelve marathons in one year? What would that schedule look like? How many pairs of shoes will I go through? What is my wife going to say?*

I did a quick search online for a comprehensive guide to all the marathon races in the United States, looked at the calendar, grabbed my credit card, and signed up for them all.

When you wait, you find reasons why you can't. Why you won't. Why you shouldn't. We need to just do.

And I was about to do:

- Carlsbad Marathon in January
- Iron Horse Trail Marathon in February
- Los Angeles Marathon in March
- San Luis Obispo Marathon in April
- Surfer's Path Marathon in May
- Rock-n-Roll Marathon (Seattle) in June
- San Francisco Marathon in July
- Santa Rosa Marathon in August
- Night Sweats Marathon in September
- Lake Tahoe Marathon in October
- New York Marathon in November
- California International Marathon in December (Double Marathon)
- New Year's One Day, a twenty-four-hour race at Crissy Field in San Francisco

My resolution is where this story started. I was determined to do more than I ever felt I was capable, to stretch, and grow in 2017—to see what I was made of. My journey—my challenge—began with running, and I don't plan to stop. I hope my story challenges you to go write your own.

Chapter One

THE FIRST ONE

Don't be too rigid with training or race preparation. Just go have fun!

The first one is always special. Whether it's a first date, first kiss, first job, first day of school, or in my case, the first run of the year, the first one always means a little more than those that follow. Some people approach that moment with more reverence or with greater preparation. Others just take the leap without overthinking it. Some confidence is necessary; too much can be detrimental.

My inaugural race to kick off 2017—and my marathon year—went something like this.

On Friday my wife and I picked up the kids from school.

"Dad, why are you here? You never pick us up from school; you're usually at work."

"Oh, I got off early today, and we're going out for an early dinner."

"Where are we going, and why are we eating so early?"

"You'll see!"

As we exited the highway, our six-year-old daughter asked, "Why are we at the airport?"

My wife and I didn't say anything. I pulled into long-term parking and turned off the car. "We're getting on a plane right now and flying down to San Diego. We're going to LEGOLAND tomorrow. And dad is running a marathon on Sunday!"

"*Woohoo!* Wait. Dad is running a marathon on Sunday? Cool!"

What the kids didn't know was there was a "Marathon Mile" at LEGOLAND for them to run Saturday morning. When I registered for the Carlsbad Marathon I discovered an offer for discounted tickets to LEGOLAND and early entry to the park. Heck, yeah!

On Saturday morning, the entire family geared up and ran a mile together (with about a thousand other families) through LEGOLAND, which was a pretty special experience. Now you may be thinking, *Why are you running a race the day before a marathon and also planning to be on your feet all day long?* I get it; this might not be the best pre-race strategy, but sometimes you have to compromise and do what's best for your family. For me, that meant spending Saturday going on almost every ride and seeing every attraction. After a long day of fun, both kids fell asleep in the car as my wife drove me to pick up my race bib, packet, and other registration goodies.

It was 6:00 p.m. I had run a mile that morning and been on my feet all day long, in the sun, and now it was time to prep for 26.2 miles. My motto is, *if you're early, you're on time; if you're on time, you're late!* So I planned to get up at 3:30 on Sunday morning, have breakfast at 4:00, and be on the shuttle to the start at 4:45, leaving plenty of time to get situated at the start. But first, we needed to get back to the hotel, clean up, and find somewhere to eat dinner that night.

I have friends who get to a marathon location two or three days before a race and don't do anything at all for those days—not even leave the hotel. My thinking is if you're so dialed in and something does go off course, it's difficult to get back on track because you're on such a regimented plan.

Sunday morning my alarm and wakeup call rang out in perfect symmetry. We were staying at the "official" race hotel for the marathon, but for some reason they didn't have an early breakfast for the runners. Like I said, I try to go with the flow. Instead of my usual oatmeal, I had some dry cereal (They only had milk and I'm a vegan.), two bananas, and a piece of bread (no toaster). Thankfully, I had a packet of almond butter for some protein.

Some marathons are *only* a marathon. And some marathons have a half-marathon attached, which is a good way for race organizers to get more people signed up, get them to the expo, and get more people in front of vendors and sponsors, products, and advertising, which creates a more festive atmosphere in general. The thing was, the marathoners don't see any of those half-marathoners because they usually have a later start time. Regardless, my focus was on *my* race, the first of the year!

In case you haven't already guessed, I signed up for the Carlsbad race feeling a little bit too confident. I'd just run my personal best marathon a month before and figured I could sail through this race without much training.

And for a while, I was sailing. But around Mile 18, things got "real"—as in really hard. We were running along the highway right above the beach, and the headwind was intense. I'd kept up with the 3:45 pace group, which had whittled down from twenty to about three runners. Any chance of blocking the wind for each other was out the door.

And then it happened.

I saw my family at Mile 19. My two children shook cowbells, and my wife gave me a big beautiful smile. Their encouragement gave my internal batteries the boost they needed. I gave them each a kiss and kept running. It doesn't matter what race it is, or what my time is, I always stop and give my family a kiss when I see them on the course.

This drives my wife nuts. She always tells me to "get a good time" or "hurry up and get back with the pack," but I don't care—their support and love matter more to me than any number.

The last seven miles were pretty rough, as they usually are, because your body is breaking down and you can smell the finish line. At that point in my training, I was still following the "Adam" not-much-training program. I hadn't yet made the full commitment and didn't fully understand what I needed to do this year. Running a marathon a month was new, and I was quickly learning it was time to step up my game.

I caught up with the 3:45 pace group, got enveloped into a huge sea of half-marathoners, rode their wave to the finish, and completed race number one of 2017 in 3:43.

What did I learn?

1. Life is unpredictable. Make your training and routines function the same way, so you can easily ebb and flow during race weekend if you have to.
2. If I was going to meet this running goal, there would definitely need to be some long runs in my training.
3. For any future marathons I run, I'll have to check to see if there's a half associated with the race. Nothing against half-marathoners, but the last miles can be very congested with so many people.
4. Smiling when it hurts and when you're tired has an awesome effect on your energy level. Smile, smile, smile!

Sunday afternoon we enjoyed some brief pool time then headed to the airport and flew home! The next marathon was twenty-seven days away.

Ideas to Consider and Share

Has there been a time when you've packed in a ton of activities before a race or activity? How did you perform? What did you learn? Did being that busy help you for next time?

Share your stories on Instagram, Facebook, Twitter, and Strava.

#RUNLAP

Chapter Two

Why?

The race starts at Mile 20. It's like
April of a school year, when all
the work comes to fruition.

For me, running is a form of mediation, sifting out the clutter to reveal the nuggets of goodness that have risen to the surface for more attention. Twelve marathons would bring all those hidden nuggets to the surface. I wanted to find more clarity and bring out what's most important in my body and mind so I could analyze it and reach my full capacity.

Running a marathon is like many aspects of life. There are ups and downs along with high energy and intense fatigue. You need friends and colleagues to help you through. And when it's all over, you can't wait to start again.

I've always hesitated to focus solely on my career because we have to focus on ourselves too. If we're not happy and healthy outside of work, we're not going to be any good when we're actually at work.

When I run 26.2 miles, it hurts, but the experience allows me to look inside my body and mind and find ideas, solutions, and capacity

I would not have otherwise been able to access. This kind of suffering brings clarity. I'd run a total of seven marathons prior to 2017, and each one forces me to hone in on minute details swirling around in my brain during a race. All other noise is pushed out because I run a long way, and only that which really matters gets revealed.

Suffering more for a year would strengthen my body but also my work as an educator, author, husband, and father. It's those moments at Mile 17, Mile 25, and during 4:00 a.m. training runs that make the reason for doing this so crystal clear for me.

Ironically, a big problem for those new to running is that they only see the finish line. They see someone wearing a medal and want one for themselves. That is true in all areas of life, not just with races but events. A neighbor has a new car or is going on vacation, and you want the same. What we don't see is all the hard work that led up to that medal, vacation, or car. We see the final result but have zero concept of what it took to get there.

I wanted to become more aware of and more intentional about what goes into accomplishing the big goals. I knew it would take hard work, more long days, more early mornings, more stress on my body and brain. That *more* was what this marathon year was all about. I wanted to find out what I had inside me—what I could really do.

#RunLAP Reflections from Barry Richburg
Principal, North Carolina, @YatesMillES

As a principal, I am often asked why I run. My students, parents, teachers, and staff wonder why I run so much and how I find time to run while leading a school each day. As I prepare to answer those questions, I reflect on my teaching experience and my administrative experience. Once I reflect on this, the answer is always easy. I run to motivate, inspire, challenge, and accomplish.

I want to motivate all of my stakeholders: my community, my students, and my teachers. I want to lead by example and show that anything is possible. I want to prove that even when we are busy and going strong to master the craft of education, we can still reach for personal goals. I want to motivate people and help them see that any goal we focus on is obtainable.

I want to inspire them to love fitness, love life, and love feeling good about themselves. I hope to inspire my students to apply this type of dedication to their course work.

As someone who loves a good challenge, running is a challenge you can set for yourself. You can challenge yourself to be better and even compete with yourself. You are the one who sets the tone and path for your destiny, so why not challenge yourself to be better? This is a message I give to my staff as well.

A number of accomplishments can be obtained through education. Running is very connected to this as you continue to achieve your running goals. In 2017, I ran twelve races for the year. As this is a big accomplishment, I am eagerly excited to run eighteen races in 2018. #18N18.

Ideas to Consider and Share

Why do you do what you do?

What is it that you're looking for in life? Have you found it?

What else do you need to do to get there?

Share your stories on Instagram, Facebook, Twitter, and Strava.

#RUNLAP

SUCCESSFUL PEOPLE
REPLACE THE WORDS
"WISH," "SHOULD," AND
"TRY" WITH "I WILL."
GO MAKE IT HAPPEN —
JUST. SAY. YES.

Chapter Three

CLARITY

Running pushes out all the noise.

It doesn't matter what you do or what you want to do. When you do what's hard, you come out the other end with clarity. You silence the noise in your life for a period of time.

Tuning out the noise that surrounds our daily lives is vitally important. How often are you alone with your thoughts? Alone without distractions, without your phone, without music, without notifications, and people vying for your attention?

Running helps me to focus on what's really important. The amplification of new ideas that rise to the surface of my mind during a run is without a doubt the most creative space I have. In the absence of a muse, running takes that place and helps me find clarity.

Mile 25 of a marathon has provided so many realizations over the years. Your body may be telling you to stop, to eat, to walk, to drink, but your brain is urging you to continue. In those moment, I can see exactly where I need to be, where I've been, and where I need to go.

It is those moments of pain, suffering, challenge, and solitude that makes it worth it. And my brain thanks me.

Ideas to Consider and Share

Where do you find clarity? Where is your thinking place? What happens for you there?

Share your stories on Instagram, Facebook, Twitter, and Strava.

Chapter Four

WANNA GO RUN?

It's only 13.1 miles; that's half as long as 26.2.

"A half marathon, for real?" I questioned. "I'm not sure, Frank. It's been two years since I put on running shoes."

"C'mon Adam, my daughter got hurt and she can't run. It'll be fun since it's on trails and also the inaugural event for The North Face."

"All right, I'm in!"

That brief exchange with my buddy Frank changed the course of my life—not just my exercise-life, my entire life.

Ideas to Consider and Share

How often do you do things on a whim? If you don't, why not? If you have, what's been the outcome? How might your encouragement improve someone else's life?

Share your stories on Instagram, Facebook, Twitter, and Strava.

#RUNLAP

SOME DAYS YOU'RE GOING TO FEEL HORRIBLE, TIRED, AND MAYBE EVEN SICK. DON'T GIVE UP, DON'T MAKE AN EXCUSE, AND DON'T PUT IT OFF. ONCE YOU START GOING, YOU'LL FEEL BETTER

Chapter Five

It Almost Never Was

Just put on some shoes and run.

December 5, 2009, was the day, and it almost never was.

Frank picked me up at dark-thirty that morning, and we made our way to the Marin Headlands for the inaugural The North Face Endurance Challenge. I knew I could run 13.1 miles; I just wasn't super excited.

It was cold and dark, and I knew the course had miles of elevation gain. Frank and I have snow skied together for years, and his stoke factor definitely rubbed off on me. By the time we arrived, my mood had taken a positive turn.

We parked, and as soon as I got out of the car, I heard my name. Allie, an old friend who turned out to be a super-fast runner, came over to say hello. She came with another friend whose name I didn't recognize, and we agreed to meet up after the race to chat some more.

Today, The North Face has become very well-known for its Endurance Challenge Race Series, but this was the first event. A buzz filled the air as runners made their way to the start and got ready to take off.

Frank and I are both notorious for being early, wherever we go. If the ski lifts open at 9:00 a.m., we get there at 7:30 a.m. This race started at 8:00 a.m., and we probably got there by 6:00 a.m. There's not much to do before a race except walk around or find a warm spot to sit. The event organizers thoughtfully placed huge industrial heaters around the start area, and many racers were huddling around trying to stay warm.

As I made my way toward the nearest heater, I spotted a lone runner, hunched down and trying desperately to warm up.

"Don't I know you?" I asked. Honestly, I was not trying to flirt with her.

"*Uhhhhh.*"

"You're Allie's friend, right?"

"Yeah, I am."

She was not too interested in talking. Her focus seemed to be on getting warm. She had a serious look on her face, and I knew that asking more questions wouldn't help.

"Okay. Well, good luck on the run!"

"Yup."

That was it. We went our separate ways, and I ran a 2:06:16 half-marathon that day.

Ideas to Consider and Share

When have you entered a race, or tried something new, and weren't totally prepared? How did it work out?

Share your stories on Instagram, Facebook, Twitter, and Strava.

#RUNLAP

Chapter Six

No, I'm Not

Remember your dreams, and forget
what other people say about them.

There's a word that gets tossed around way too often, usually in reference to something a person has done, or a big idea they're hoping to accomplish. We use it as a way to describe our lives, daily situations we're involved in, and in my opinion, this word inhibits our growth as human beings.

To be honest, people use this word to describe me all the time. Before 2017, I didn't really think much of it. I'm sure I probably used the word on occasion as well and didn't give it a second thought. Since then I have a big problem with this word.

I'm just going to say it.

I am not *crazy.*

And what I do isn't crazy.

I'm not an addict, either. I'm not chasing down a dream that my parents wanted for me. I'm simply maximizing my full potential as a human in a way that energizes me. Crazy has nothing to do with it.

Squeezing out every ounce of potential that's inside your body—that is what life is about. You're crazy if you don't.

Here are a few responses I heard during my marathon year:

Me: "I'm going to bed at nine tonight and then going to wake up at midnight to run ten miles?"

Others: *That's crazy!*

Me: "This year I'm going to eat vegan and see if it helps with recovery for all my races?"

Others: *Why would you do that? What are you going to eat, salad? Totally crazy!*

Me: "I'm going to finish off the year with one more event, a twenty-four-hour race on New Year's Eve."

Others: *I could never do that. So crazy!*

But I have a few questions for all the "others": How do you know? Have you tried it? Has the idea ever entered your brain as an option? Do you know anyone who's done it?

We often put arbitrary limits on ourselves without even taking the first step. It makes me upset to think about all the missed opportunities—times that people waited on the sidelines and never walked onto the field or the trail. What is it that holds people back and doesn't allow them to move forward with new, big, and bold ideas?

I believe you can move forward. I believe you should. And I believe you must. We all must. Bold and big ideas push us out of the comfort zone. You're not growing, failing, or learning in that comfort zone.

When I was a little boy in elementary school, physical education (PE) was my favorite subject. The games we played were the highlights I shared during dinner each night. One of my most vivid memories happened in third grade.

I was a pretty good athlete and enjoyed playing sports and being part of a team. What I didn't love to do was run—especially when we ran the mile.

It's funny how some things don't change. I enjoy running to this day, but I wouldn't say I love it. I'm not the most talented. I get super tired during races, and some days, it's hard to get my butt out the door for training, but I always put in the work and get it done.

Back to third grade. We had run the mile a few times that year and were coming up on final grades for our report card. The last run of the year was about a month away, and my PE teacher called me aside for a chat.

"Adam, I always see you running and sweating and giving it 100 percent in my PE class. Way to go."

"Oh wow, thanks a lot, Coach!"

"You can do better! You have more inside. I know it!"

My PE teacher in third grade saw something I didn't. He knew there was more and threw down the gauntlet for me to find it. *Game on!*

"I want you to try to run a sub-six-minute mile next month."

My mind started racing. My fastest time was somewhere around 6:30, and I was tired when I crossed the finish line. Done. Nothing left in the tank. But my teacher believed in me.

Later that night at dinner, I told my parents about what he said. They asked me one question.

"We believe you can do it, Adam, but do *you* believe?"

Having others believe in you is important. But you must first believe in yourself. When you're doing something difficult, they aren't out there with you. You aren't thinking about them when you're tired, frustrated, thirsty, cold, hungry, lost, and wanting to give up.

A month later, I crossed the line of that final mile run at 5:57. I'd done it. I ran so hard I couldn't speak. My lungs burned, and I started throwing up. But I'd done it. My teacher believed in me, my parents knew I could, and the only person able to stop me was me.

Don't call me crazy. I just happen to like bold ideas. Deep down, I bet you do too.

#RunLAP Reflections from Jay Posick
Middle School Principal, Wisconsin, @posickj

I am an educator who runs. I love running and have run every day since August 30, 1987. I ran on my wedding day, my daughter's birthday, on days when we've celebrated the life of a relative or friend. I have participated in twenty-nine marathons, including running the races in New York once, Boston twice, and Chicago three times. At the time of this writing, I am days away from running my thirtieth marathon, the Twin Cities Marathon, one for each year of my streak.

I started my running streak while I was coaching volleyball at my alma mater. I ran track at Marquette University, but when I was working out with the volleyball players, I noticed that I couldn't keep up with them. Later, I coached middle school track and cross country, and I ran with those athletes during every practice. Running became a part of my regular routine.

So why do I continue to run? There are two reasons that really stick out for me: my mental health and being a role model for my family and school. Being an educator and coach is not necessarily conducive to a healthy lifestyle. Late nights, fast food, skipping meals, early mornings, and long bus rides aren't the best thing for your body. Having a chance to run, either alone or with friends, allowed me to clear my head, think about situations at home or school, and set goals for my life. Running has helped me find time for me, something only I can do, and it has helped maintain my sanity even on the toughest days.

Students, staff, and families know about my running streak and are often amazed by it. We have conversations about how it started and why it continues, but most often, the discussion turns to marathons. Running my first marathon was awesome, but the Friday before my last Chicago marathon, without my knowledge, the principal had all of the students file through the office to give me high fives. Just days before my 10,000th straight day, the entire school planned an assembly to celebrate with me and my family.

Running has kept me going strong as a husband, father, and educator. It's been so long (more than thirty years) that I don't even know what I would do without my daily run. I guess you could say that running has been my buried treasure, but I sure like sharing it with others.

Ideas to Consider and Share

What's something you've done or wanted to do that people said was "crazy," but you didn't listen to them? How can you continue moving forward with your dreams and goals even when others say you can't?

Share your stories on Instagram, Facebook, Twitter, and Strava.

#RUNLAP

YOU MAY THINK YOU HAVE LIMITS, BUT YOU REALLY DON'T. DON'T IMPOSE THEM, DON'T LISTEN TO THEM; CROSS THE LINE AND KEEP ON GOING.

Chapter Seven

Dad, Did You Win?

**First or last, it doesn't matter.
Go enter the race.**

Without fail, whenever I get home from a marathon, my son, Tilden, always asks me, "Dad, did you win?"

It always makes me smile one of those smiles that permeates the outside and the inside as well. I really can't remember when it started, and at first, my wife and I would giggle because it was just so stinkin' cute. The first time he asked, I almost said, "Are you serious?" But I quickly remembered he was just a little guy and had no concept of the thousands of runners in the race. The innocence of it all was really special, and over time, I tried to put myself into his four-year-old brain and understand what he was thinking.

How must I look in his eyes if he wants me to win and thinks I can? When dad runs and the schedule permits, the entire family comes out. They make signs, bring the cowbells, go to the expo, and always want to eat my runner food if they have a chance. I'm his dad, and he looks up to me. The entire experience is sweet.

More than that, though, my wife and I really feel that exposing our kids to competition is important. We don't necessarily talk about "winning." Our focus is on working hard. Giving 100 percent is the standard we've established in the Welcome household.

Last February, I was signed up to run the Buzz Marathon in Central California, which actually takes place on a US Army base. We've driven by the base a hundred times over the years, and it looked like a really fun place to run a marathon. About three weeks before race day, my wife asked one of those "Honey, can we look at the calendar together, please?" questions.

That's code for there's something she wants to change and we need to talk. My February marathon happened to fall on President's Day weekend, and when I showed Stacy my original calendar, there weren't any red flags. But that was before Lake Tahoe had one of the biggest snowfalls in history, and she wanted to go skiing with the family. Fair enough, right? California had been in a multi-year drought, and the snow had been pretty bad for several seasons.

We had a problem, or more accurately, *I had a problem*. Of course, I wanted to go skiing. We'd just bought brand new skis, and I wanted to try them out on the epic snow that had just been dumped in Lake Tahoe. But I also needed to find a marathon in February that could substitute the one I'd already registered for, in order to keep pace with my one-marathon-a-month goal.

After a quick search online, there weren't any marathons in California that could fit on the calendar and only a few others that were happening in Alabama, Arkansas, and some other east coast state. At first, I suggested my wife ski with the kids without me. That didn't go over well. And truthfully I wanted to do both.

After thinking about the dilemma for about twelve minutes, I decided to compromise. *Heck, yeah! Let's go skiing for four days! I can create and run my own marathon instead.* At the end of the day, what did it really matter? This was my goal, I wasn't competing against anyone, there weren't any leaderboards, and I was accountable to myself.

So that's exactly what I did. I chose a different weekend in February, had a couple of friends run the first few miles with me, and then ran 26.2 on the trail by my house. I wore my GPS the entire time, was totally legit on the time, and carried everything I needed along the way. My family met me for the last six miles of the marathon. My wife ran next to me, and our kids rode their bikes. The experience was fantastic in so many ways, and I ran a 3:45 marathon that day.

But the best part of the day was this conversation:

"Hey, Tilden! Guess what?"

"What, Dad?"

"I just won that race!"

We all started laughing at our inside joke, and I was again reminded how important it is to include family in our passions and adventures and to keep things fun, so these activities become lifelong endeavors.

In hindsight, I'm really glad we were able to go skiing because the snow was absolutely amazing that year, and my two young kids were totally shredding all over the mountain. And I learned a little bit more about myself.

Don't take things too seriously.

Make concessions to benefit the entire family. Family time always wins.

Working out and racing is important, especially to be an example to your kids. But it's more important to show them flexibility and that family comes first.

Running an organized marathon is fun, but running your own marathon is also fun—and you can do it on your schedule! Just get some friends to run a few miles with you, and get it done!

Ideas to Consider and Share

Has there been a time you needed to be flexible with training or a race? What happened? How did you react? Did it turn into a learning moment?

Share your stories on Instagram, Facebook, Twitter, and Strava.

#*RUNLAP*

Chapter Eight

JUST. START.

Put on some shoes and run. If you don't
have shoes, run barefoot in the grass.

There's too much planning and not enough doing. Just start.

Too many people shopping for the right gear. Just start.

Way too many conversations about that equipment that you don't even need. Just start.

Too much looking at other people's training plans. Just start.

What day of the week is my long run, speed workout, or rest day? Just start.

Where should I go? Who should I go with? What should I wear? Should I start next week or January 1? Just start.

You don't need a plan. Throw on some shoes, and start moving your legs. Just start.

Dean Karnazes didn't have a detailed plan when he made his now-famous run to Half Moon Bay in the middle of the night. He just started running.

You don't need to buy a magazine or a training manual. Just start.

Don't fear failure and loss. Embrace what you'll learn and discover when you try again, try again, try again, and try again!

I believe in you. I know you can do it. I know you will be successful. I know you will figure it out. If you start.

Back in 2006, a friend of mine was talking about running a marathon. I was teaching third grade at the time and working at a running shoe store on the weekends, so this conversation wasn't totally abnormal. What *was* abnormal was my name in the conversation and hitting the "register" button for the marathon later that afternoon.

I haven't always relied on planning and thinking things through in my life. If an idea sounds good and it seems feasible to attain, then I might as well go do it.

Well, this marathon I registered for was happening in three weeks. As in twenty-one days. And I hadn't been running any distance over a 5K, nor had I ever run more than three miles at any time in my life.

So what did I do? I threw myself into some training, read a bunch of articles, booked a hotel room, and went to the marathon—alone.

My friend flaked three days before the race. He hadn't "trained' enough" to run 26.2 miles. Well, I hadn't either, but once you register for a race and tell yourself you're running, there's no reason to stop the achievement from happening.

Running that marathon was an amazing experience. I can remember the cheering crowds, all the homemade signs, ringing cowbells, bands playing every few miles, and how completely trashed my body was afterwards.

But I didn't think about my body and lack of training during the race. I was absorbing the energy of the crowds, thinking about the finish line, and watching the other runners who probably hadn't trained enough either. And I finished. With a time of 3:57, no less.

On the way back to my car, which was parked at the hotel, I had to stop about fifty times to rest—and it was only a few blocks away. I would have called a taxi for a ride but hadn't put any cash in my key pocket. And you know what? I loved every step.

Don't ever let anyone tell you that you can't, that you're not prepared enough, that you don't look like a runner, or that you have the wrong shoes.

Listen to your gut and your instincts. Listen to that voice inside that's telling you, "Yes you can. Yes you should!"

Ideas to Consider and Share

How can you keep things simple and just start doing? Have you? What was the result?

Share your stories on Instagram, Facebook, Twitter, and Strava.

 #RUNLAP

NO ONE CAN STOP YOU FROM DOING SOMETHING YOU ARE DETERMINED TO DO.

Chapter Nine

THAT ONE DAY

**I don't like tests, but I pass
the important ones.**

Remember that girl I met before the chilly half marathon in 2009? There's more to the story.

I got home from the race and searched the results to find out who she was and what her time had been. First off, she beat me! Second, she was older—by six years. I wanted to meet her. Even though she wasn't exactly friendly before the race, I just had a feeling.

So I emailed our mutual friend. I began with the usual banter, "Hello, it was great to see you. How was your race?" (She won the entire thing.) Then I inquired about her friend. Basically, I told Allie that if Stacy was single, I wanted to take her out.

A couple of hours later, not that I was checking every three minutes, the email response finally arrived.

"She is single, and I just got off the phone with her. She wants to go out with you too!"

This was Sunday, December 5, 2009. Allie sent over Stacy's phone number, and I called her that night. We chatted on the phone briefly, talking about the race and our careers. I suggested we meet that Thursday and take the train into San Francisco for the evening. In my typical style, our first date was planned, and I had no idea what would come next.

From where we lived, the train ride to San Francisco took about thirty-five minutes. The plan was to take her to the Museum of Modern Art to view some of their new installations and then have dinner at the Ferry Building.

Conversation on the train was going well, she was easy to talk with, and we found lots of commonalities. And then it happened. Less than ninety minutes into our first date, walking up the staircase to the museum, she asked, "You're pretty intense, aren't you?"

At first I didn't know what to say. Yes, I have opinions. I'm strong willed. "I want what I want and am not going to settle for something that I don't," I blurted.

A big smile came across Stacy's face, and we continued up the stairs.

The museum was great. Some of my favorite paintings in the world were on display, and I could tell Stacy was enjoying it as well. We continued on to the Ferry Building and found a great place to eat overlooking the water. That's where we realized we were both vegetarians, and the connection between us grew a little bit stronger.

We were sitting at the bar for dinner, so we were side by side. And then it happened. She put her hand on my leg. I knew this woman was something special, and I didn't want the evening to end. We were both runners (I was actually more of a cyclist at the time), shared the same political viewpoints, both had a parent who was battling cancer, and I know we both had a "feeling" about each other.

The night ended, and we stayed in touch. Actually we never were out of touch because we got married one-hundred days after that first date. Believe what you want about fate and stars aligning, but I truly believe that my buddy Frank was supposed to invite me to that race, where I didn't even want to run, and I was supposed to meet Stacy in front of that heater. We were supposed to create this wonderful life that we have together.

In our marriage vows, we promised to always run together, and we still do to this day!

Ideas to Consider and Share

If you have a cool story about meeting your partner at a race or during your favorite activity, please share!

Share your stories on Instagram, Facebook, Twitter, and Strava.

#RUNLAP

YOU MIGHT BE IN SOME
DARK PLACES FROM TIME
TO TIME AND THAT'S OKAY.
EVERYTHING THAT IS GOOD
WAS MEANT TO BE HARD.
KEEP RUNNING TOWARD
THE LIGHT; IT'S OUT THERE.

Chapter Ten

Do What's Hard

Easy doesn't get you to your goals; hard does.

Doing what's easy is no fun, no work, and carries such little reward. Do what's hard.

If you're always doing what's easy, when things get hard, they're *really* going to be hard.

Easy doesn't help you grow, easy doesn't get you that next step; easy keeps you in the same spot where you already are.

Hard gets you moving, hard gets you growing, hard gets you reflecting, and hard makes it worth it.

If we're always doing what's easy and avoiding the hard, how can we expect our kids to react when it's hard?

If yesterday didn't work for you, tomorrow is a second chance. Don't make it easy.

The more we do what's hard, the more we do what takes work, and the easier most things become.

Hard reminds you that you're living, hard reminds you to grow, and hard reminds you to wake up and get out of bed each morning.

It's not always going to be easy. Actually, most of the time, it's going to be the complete opposite of easy. What is the point of taking the easy way? There's no challenge with easy. There's not much you can learn with easy. You can't get inside your brain with easy.

Easy may get you across the finish line (when it's easy), but what about when it's hard? I'm training for those hard moments. I'm getting ready for the pain. For the time when my body says "No more" but my brain has a different agenda.

Don't think small and easy. Tell yourself what you're going to do, and you'll do it.

"But Adam, how do I even get my mind in that space to think bigger, bolder, and harder?"

You must put yourself in situations that make you nervous. They may just have you second-guessing yourself and not quite sure if you'll be standing when it's all over. If you don't get to that place, you will never know what's on the other side.

So let me make something clear. I'm not especially brave. I simply go forward.

In April of 2017, I was quickly approaching marathon number three in my twelve-race year. Some months were much easier to schedule than others. April was not one of those easy months. The number of marathons was pretty scarce, and it was busy time for the family.

It just so happened that I was going to be in Palm Springs for a conference during the middle of the month, and the Los Angeles marathon was happening that very same weekend. It worked out even better that we were flying down late Wednesday evening, and the conference ended on Saturday afternoon. I could attend the conference and then find my way over to Los Angeles, which was only a two-hour drive.

The first couple of days of the conference went well. I had some early morning shake-out runs in Palm Springs—a few miles to keep the legs lively. Did I mention my idea to (somehow) charter a helicopter to fly from Palm Springs to Los Angeles? A week earlier, I even mentioned it to my wife. She gave me one of those are-you-serious-about-taking-a-helicopter looks, and the next question was about the price.

Turns out it costs $2,500 for a forty-five minute helicopter ride. In my mind, *I'm doing it!* In my wife's mind, *not a chance.* Fair enough.

For thirty-five dollars, I grabbed a rental car at the airport and drove over without a hitch. If you've never been to Los Angeles, driving there is pretty intense. The city itself is huge, there's always tons of traffic, construction, and always a lot going on.

I arrived in Los Angeles around 1:00 p.m. on Saturday and still had to grab my bib at the expo, which wasn't too far from the hotel. But this was LA, and it takes time to do everything. The parking lot for the expo was a massive complex, it took thirty minutes to find a spot and enter the expo, then another forty-five minutes to drive back to the hotel. (For some context, I could have run from the expo to the hotel in about fifteen minutes.) Then I had to return my rental car, check into the hotel, grab something to eat, and get ready for the marathon.

By the time I was ready for race day, had everything laid out, and was able to get in bed, it was around 9:30 p.m.—which is pretty late for me the night before a race. I had woken in Palm Springs at a conference that morning, driven over the mountains from the desert into the big city, and would run 26.2 miles the next day.

Turns out the hotel (an official race hotel) didn't have an early breakfast option like they usually do, and the Starbucks across the street didn't open until 6:00 a.m., which was way too late. Things don't always go as planned.

The next morning, my 4:00 a.m. alarm went off, and I downed a CLIF Bar® along with two bananas and a bagel with some almond butter, which was the breakfast of choice with the limited options. Thankfully there was a late checkout, so I would be able to shower at the hotel after the race before heading to the airport and my flight home. Speaking of my flight: I didn't have much time to catch it after the race. But first, let's run this marathon!

I grabbed the bus to Dodger Stadium and had about ninety minutes to chill out until things got underway. With big races like this, they often have different starting gates. At registration, racers entered their estimated finishing time in order to assign racers to the appropriate gate. Somehow I was placed in the back, and there wasn't any opportunity to move forward because of security.

In my head, I told myself it was okay, but I considered the consequences of being in the back of the pack. I always like running with a pace group during marathons. They help keep you on track, and it's a fun way to meet other runners that are your speed. This wasn't going to happen today.

When the race started, I sprinted. I sprinted and bobbed and weaved and squeezed my way through the horde of people in front of me. And it was the stupidest thing I've ever done. A marathon is a marathon for a reason; it's 26.2 miles. And you can't sprint the first couple of miles and expect to run smoothly for the remainder of the race.

I caught the group at Mile 2 and actually settled into a nice little groove. The pacer was a great guy who'd flown out from Ohio for the race. At Mile 13, the wheels fell off.

The late nights with friends at the conference, the early mornings for shakeout runs, and the drive from Palm Springs took their toll on my energy stores. So I stopped running. I didn't stop moving, I just started to walk. And process. And regroup my body to reassess what I needed to do in order to finish this race—and catch my flight home.

It looked like I may miss my flight if it took six hours to finish this race. And Todd, my *Kids Deserve It* podcast partner, and I had an appointment at the airport to record an episode thirty minutes before my flight boarded!

The number one rule to keep in mind during stressful situations: don't stress out. Regroup and allow your training to take over, which will inevitably get you across the finish line. I drank some water, looked around, and remembered all the training I'd done. Thinking about my family put a huge smile on my face, and I started to run again—slowly.

When running a marathon, run your race. It's even more important to run your race when you're at Mile 13 and you need to regroup just to cross the finish line.

As the miles ticked off, I didn't necessarily feel amazing, but I started to feel better. I was reminded that I'm out here for fun; this goal of running one marathon a month for an entire year was my idea. I started this journey because I wanted to experience pain, to suffer, and do something that was outside of anything I'd previously done.

I was getting exactly what I asked for and more, and the smile on my face got even bigger!

I trudged across the finish line in 4:03. I finished, and not too far off my original goal of 3:45. It wasn't pretty, but it didn't need to be. Most importantly, I'd learned so much about myself. When you think you're done, dig a little deeper and see what you have inside.

When we do what's hard, whether we plan on it or not, we come out stronger—and smarter—on the other side.

I made it back to my hotel and to the airport, and we recorded our podcast just minutes before my flight boarded. I was exhausted, but I was home.

You have it in you. You have it in you today. You have it in you tomorrow. You have it in you next week. Do something that's hard, something you never thought you could finish, and see what happens.

Keep your focus in line, channel stress into energy so you make sound decisions, and see how you come out on the other end.

Anything you really want to do in life is going to be hard.

Go get after it!

Ideas to Consider and Share

What have you done that was hard? How did you prepare? How did you react? How did it change you after it was all said and done?

Share your stories on Instagram, Facebook, Twitter, and Strava.

#RUNLAP

Chapter Eleven

GET UP EARLIER

You can always take a power nap later.

I can't tell you how many people I talk with on a daily basis who say they just don't have time to pursue their challenge of choice.

"When do you work out? My schedule is too busy!"

"I just don't know how you do it with kids and everything. There are so many activities."

"The intention is always there but that snooze button. You know what I'm talking about."

You need to get up earlier, starting tomorrow.

Maybe I'm an early riser because of the newspaper route I had as a kid. Bu the morning is absolutely the best time to work out, and it's imperative to develop some type of routine to create good habits. If something is important, you will make time and sacrifice. If it's not, you won't. Here's some practical advice for tackling the important.

On a typical day, I get up at 4:00 a.m., drink a glass of water, eat some oatmeal, hop on the computer to check in on the world, get dressed for my run, and head out the door. Over the years, I've trained my brain to live and breathe this mantra: "We get up early and work out."

I feel better when I work out in the morning. I feel more accomplished knowing the entire day is ahead of me. I feel happier after having a good sweat. I know that no matter what happens that day, others can't take away the experience and how amazing my body feels. Pushing myself to get up early, to run every day no matter what, is how I run like a pirate.

Adam's Tips for Getting Up Early

- Tell yourself repeatedly the day before that, when the alarm clock goes off, you're not going to hit snooze, and you're getting up immediately.
- Always set two alarms, a few minutes apart.
- When you're starting this routine, put the alarm clock just out of reach from your bed, so you must get up and turn it off.
- Flash forward to when your workout is done. Think about how amazing you're going to feel.
- Find some accountability partners on social media or via text. Nobody ever wants to say, "Workout failed; I couldn't get out of bed."
- Go to bed earlier. Set a "go to bed" alarm at night and listen to it.
- Have a "no television, laptop, or device" rule after dinner. Lying in bed with a device is bad for so many reasons and almost always keeps you up longer.
- Put out all the gear you're going to need the night before. I leave mine in the kitchen in a nice little pile with everything I need. When it's all there in front of you, it's another nice reminder in the morning.
- Don't complain about getting up early; celebrate it.

The pirate gets up early. The pirate puts in the hustle. The pirate puts in the work. The pirate enjoys the morning grind. The pirate enjoys the sweat—even when he or she wants to stay in bed!

Ideas to Consider and Share

When do you work out? Any tips to share for getting up early? Post some photos from a super early workout and help motivate the #RunLAP community!

Share your stories on Instagram, Facebook, Twitter, and Strava.
#RUNLAP

PEOPLE ASK ME ALL THE TIME WHAT I'M TRAINING FOR. I TELL THEM LIFE. THAT'S MY RACE, AND I KEEP TRAINING, SO I WIN.

Chapter Twelve

Two in a Row

Get back up. Nobody may be there to
help you, but find a way to get back up.

I had exactly five weeks in between marathons, and I reassessed
my training to see if anything could improve.

My training could always be tweaked, of course—some additional
long runs, speed work, and probably some more rest days would do
my body a favor. But my diet seemed pretty dialed in, and I wasn't
sure what could change.

I've been a vegetarian for about ten years, and in 2017, I decided,
in addition to running a bunch of marathons, I would also eat vegan.
To tell you the truth, this was something I'd been rolling around in
my brain for about a year. The biggest factor for a vegan diet is the
recovery time with running. You get a lot less inflammation in your
joints when you don't eat animal products, and I'd already seen the
results with some really fast recovery after my previous marathons.
Confident with my updated diet, I changed my training up a little bit
and got ready for the next race.

Marathon number four for the year was in San Luis Obispo. The course looked spectacular, and we happened to visit San Luis Obispo every year because my wife did her undergraduate work at Cal Poly.

About a month before the race, I checked out their website and noticed they needed pacers. I emailed the person in charge and offered to pace the 3:45 group. I'd never paced before, and being a former elementary school principal, leading is something I enjoy.

I should have known when I checked in to my hotel that the weekend was going to be "interesting." There are a bunch of hotels in town, but nothing is too fancy. But for some reason, the room I got was the Honeymoon Suite. It had tall ceilings, smelled like roses, and was just kind of funny to be in. My family didn't come down for this race, so it was just me in the giant suite.

The weather was unseasonably hot, so I tried to stay hydrated and not get into a deficit, which can be difficult to rebound from. Race morning was typical, except that the race directors delayed the start by almost forty-five minutes. This may not seem like a big deal, but when you're running a marathon and you've eaten certain foods at certain times in the morning, it can really throw you off.

Once we got rolling, our group of 3:45 marathoners settled in, and it was fun being a pacer. There was another guy who had pacing duties with me, and it felt really great being able to guide others through a marathon, especially with a specific finishing time in mind. Now I'm not a local, but I know the area pretty well, so the course didn't really have any surprises.

We were clicking off miles, the group was staying together, and the mood was positive. When you pace a group, it's always important to stay at an even time. With that being said, there were a few steep hills around Mile 12, and the back half of the course went by several wineries with some rolling hills. We were ahead of schedule early in the race. Then we hit Mile 15.

The winery portion of the marathon had begun, and it was completely exposed with no shade. That forty-five-minute delay at the start was really starting to bite us. And for the second race in a row, my wheels fell off. I could feel it coming on the previous mile, but I drank some water and tried to push the feelings out. I knew if I slowed down, I would be done with the pace group. At the time, there were only a few runners left as they'd been slowly dropping from the relentless hills in the midday sun.

I had to walk. My legs were burning, and I had the chills. Whenever I run a marathon, even though there are always plenty of aid stations, I always carry a handheld water bottle. Having the chills told me I was on the verge of dehydration, and because of the heat, I'd already drained my bottle. After walking a quarter mile, I started running again and rolled into the aid station at Mile 18, desperately in need of some fluids and a refill to my bottle.

I wasn't paying much attention as I approached, but there were quite a few people just kind of hanging around. Not spectators, but runners.

"They're out of water!"

What? *How can a marathon be out of water? It's Mile 18!* We still had eight more miles to run, which may not seem like a lot, but those miles are always tough, especially in the heat.

The volunteers said water would be arriving any minute, but I didn't care. The clock was ticking, I'd already been dropped by the pace group that I was supposed to be leading. And I was still carrying that 3:45 pace sign, even though I was no longer a member.

I felt low. I felt ashamed. I felt beyond tired and exhausted. I felt like this entire year of running was a sham. *How the heck would I run another eight marathons this year?*

So I remembered.

I remembered why I started this journey in the first place and why I was at Mile 18 of a marathon with no water and very little sustenance left in my body. I'd asked for this, and I was getting exactly what I wanted.

I was suffering. I was searching for that untapped potential I knew was there. I was truly looking inside my body for what I was made of—what was deep down inside and would never have come to the surface unless I'd put myself in this very situation. You're never going to know how much capacity you actually have unless you crack open the interior of your soul and expose it to the world. Or, in this case, to the burning asphalt.

One foot in front of the other for the next eight miles and I crossed the finish line. I was still carrying the 3:45 pacer sign, and I did so with pride. I could have dropped it in a ditch miles back, but that would have been the ultimate defeat. The slowest time I'd ever run in a marathon was 4:20 and thirty-five minutes behind the pace group I was supposed to lead. Did I feel a sense of failure to the group? Of course, I did. But I walked to my car with my head held high and changed into dry clothes for the three-hour drive home.

Two really tough marathons in a row was a hard pill to swallow. But we don't give up. We learn from each race and reassess for next time. A next time to improve. That's why I run. To see what I have inside and become stronger for the next time. There is always a next time.

MARATHON
#RaceSLO
#RaceSLO
MARATHON
SAN LUIS OBISPO CA
SLO MARATHON + HALF 2017
SLO
MARATHON
+HALF 2017
SAN LUIS OBISPO
CALIFORNIA

Ideas to Consider and Share

When have you had some disappointment and how did you react?
How did you bounce back? What did you learn from the experience?

Share your stories on Instagram,
Facebook, Twitter, and Strava.

#RUNLAP

Chapter Thirteen

ACCOMPLISHMENT REGRET

Experiencing pain is the gateway to greatness!

I often try to flash forward years and even decades in my mind to think about where I'm going to be and what I want to accomplish without having any regret.

There are certain activities and goals that carry a higher degree of accomplishment during certain times of life. "Accomplishment regret planning" can help to alleviate future disappointment.

On the surface, intentionally going through suffering may seem insane. But when you involve your entire body and mind in an endeavor and share it publicly, you can only grow as a human being. The experiences you go through along the way, the people you meet, the thoughts in your brain, the highs and lows—they've led me to a profound realization.

I don't want any regret.

More energy. More pain. More smiles. More patience. More laughter. More races. More time for family. More time for me. That's what I want.

One more step. One more commitment. One more connection. One more minute reading. One more friend to connect with. One more run. More. That's what I want.

When I thought I was done, I realized there was more inside me. When I was tired, exhausted, had sore muscles, and wanted to sleep—I found more energy to expend. When I was making dinner, doing laundry, or cleaning the house and one of my kids wanted to play, I found a way to do both.

When I didn't think there was time to write another book, send another sticker, collaborate with others from around the country, I did. I discovered I had more.

I challenge you to do more. And find more to do. Focus more on a passion or challenge you've been avoiding.

If you don't try to do more, there's no way you ever will. Don't have accomplishment regret—that's an ache that stays with you.

What's your plan?

Ideas to Consider and Share

What have you wanted to do but haven't yet? And why? The time is now. Share your goal and come up with a plan. The #RunLAP community will help to hold you accountable.

Share your stories on Instagram, Facebook, Twitter, and Strava.

#RUNLAP

Chapter Fourteen

Don't Do, So I Can Do

Just because others binge watch TV, doesn't mean you have to.

For years I've heard the excuse. It's always a little different but has similar tones whenever it comes up. I used to go along with people and nod my head or give that "I understand" expression on my face, but those days are over.

People are in charge of their lives and in charge of what they do with their time. Nobody is dictating how you spend your time, how often you do something, with what regularity, with whom, or when and where. If you're pointing a finger and it's not at yourself, then something needs to change.

I always tell people I have thirty hours in a day. Some of it comes from being super-efficient with my time, planning ahead for daily tasks that are routine, or working together as a family, so we all pitch in, and Mom and Dad aren't stuck with all the chores. The key is to focus on your strengths. Forget about your weaknesses, exploit the places where you shine, and maximize that potential.

But I'm going to tell you the biggest secret of all.

It doesn't cost any money. You don't need to enroll in a self-help course to uncover the magic. Hiring a life coach isn't necessary. You simply need to decide what's really important in your life and put your energy towards those goals.

There is a lot I don't do, so I can do what I really want to. Don't let life get in the way and then use it as an excuse.

I run when I'd rather be home with my family. Sometimes our family time has to wait if we haven't gotten our workout. Maybe that seems selfish, but I can tell you that I'm much happier and more productive after a run—and that's a win for our family.

Try your best to include the family in your workout. My wife and I pushed our kids for thousands of miles in our running strollers, so we could all be together as a family. When our oldest—our daughter—turned three years old, we worked hard, so she could ride a bike and the same for our son. Now they're six and four and can ride their bikes up to fifteen miles with us, so we can be together.

I can't tell you who won the NBA championships last year or even the Super Bowl. If I did, I wouldn't have time to run. It's a choice. Don't let your *true* passion lay idle.

#RunLAP Reflections from Emily Libbert
Middle School Science Teacher, Missouri, @EmilyLibbert

You don't need perfect. You don't need fancy or expensive. You don't need more time or a slower schedule. You don't need a new season or a new year. You don't need a nicer day, warmer weather, or perfect conditions. You just need to start right now. That's it. Just start where you are, with what you have, with the busy schedule you have.

You won't get more time. In fact, your time is now less than you had just a second ago. Think about how long you have said you'd start when you had more time. How's that working?

It won't be easy. It won't be pretty. But if you keep at it, I promise it will be a beautiful transformation.

Don't compare yourself to anyone else. Just compare yourself to where you were last week.

Life doesn't get easier or slower. I just started making time. So now it's your turn.

Ideas to Consider and Share

What's something you've let go, so you have more time for yourself? What is something you could let go to make more time?

Share your stories on Instagram, Facebook, Twitter, and Strava.

DON'T DO EASY;
DO IMPACTFUL,
DO MEANINGFUL,
DO HARD,
DO WHAT'S RIGHT,
DO WHAT MAKES
YOU UNCOMFORTABLE—
DO THAT AND THEN SO
MUCH MORE.

Chapter Fifteen

THE JOGGER

**If you want your kids to participate,
then bring them along.**

"**I** used to run all the time, but it all stopped when we had kids."
"I don't know how other people do it; our kids absolutely consume us."

If you're a parent of young kids and have said something like those comments above, let me introduce you to an amazing invention: the jogging stroller (a child's stroller that is built for running). I vividly remember us checking them out online before our first child was born. We read the reviews, compared options, and wondered which one would go the fastest. When our daughter was born, we had absolutely zero intention of stopping what we loved to do. We *are* runners, and our children were going to come with us.

That first jogger went everywhere. When my wife couldn't run postpartum, we'd go on fifteen-mile walks around town. Neighbors would see us far from home, think our car had broken down, and offer us a ride. "No thanks, we're just on a walk together with Greta!"

I'd run after work and on the weekends and always bring Greta along in the jogger. It was a great bonding time for us as well. I'd tell her about the run and our surroundings, and if we saw a hawk or coyote, we'd talk about all of it. Early on, it was me talking and her listening.

When you begin a habit early on with kids, it becomes all they really know. If your habit is watching lots of television and letting your children play video games, then that's what they'll know. My wife and I wanted them to not just "know" running, but love being outdoors—even in the rain.

Life with the jogger was great; Greta was about to turn six months old and then came our first half-marathon together. Babies are actually too little to ride in the jogger, but there's a contraption that attaches a car seat to the jogger. *Yeah, let's just add another fifteen pounds for some resistance training!*

Now it may seem like a big deal to run that far pushing a jogger, but we'd done so many training runs together; it was really just another run together in early 2014. But when that race started, my adrenaline took over, and I didn't care what I was pushing or pulling. I wanted to beat the person in front of me. My wife and I were running together, and I was *theoretically* in better shape, since she had a baby almost six months earlier, but her training had ramped, and she's a go-getter when it comes to races.

We started passing people around Mile 5 and started to get some "looks" from other runners. We felt strong, so we kept a solid pace, and I gave her the let's-run-faster-because-we're-passing-lots-of-people-pushing-this-jogger look. Unsurprisingly, she gave me the let's-do-this-honey look. Game on!

Around Mile 10, it happened. At first, I thought he was joking. But it soon became evident this comment was not a joke.

"Whatever, Dude; it's so much easier to run fast when you're pushing one of those baby jogger things. You get lots of momentum, and it helps pull you faster."

Then another runner, only a few miles from the finish, accused me of running faster because I was pushing a jogger. For real? The jogger itself was thirty pounds, my daughter was about fifteen pounds, and that car seat thing my wife made us bring weighed around fifteen more. And did I mention we brought a change of clothes for after the race? We're talking about between sixty and seventy extra pounds. And don't forget, when you run pushing a stroller, your arms can't swing, and it throws off your gait. I was mad.

So what did we do? We ran faster. We were probably running eight-minute miles at that point and took the pace to around 7:45 and dropped that guy. I glanced backed to revel in his pain. I wanted to see the look on his face as we motored ahead while pushing our jogger with a six-month-old strapped in. I leaned over and whispered to my daughter, "People may talk trash to you someday. We don't talk trash back; we let our actions talk for us, and that's enough."

We crossed the finish line of our first half-marathon as a family in 1:37. There was a 5K going on at the same time, and the race officials tried to push us through that finishing line, but I wouldn't have it. We'd run 13.1 miles, and we were going to finish with those runners!

Having someone accuse me of having an advantage while pushing a jogger happened again and again during races. I still marvel that someone could actually think that was true.

Ideas to Consider and Share

Have you pushed a jogger, ridden a bike with a kid on your back, or carried a backpack with your kids?

Share your stories on Instagram,
Facebook, Twitter, and Strava.

#RUNLAP

Chapter Sixteen

STRIP DOWN

It's time to go Barney style, like *The Flintstones.*

When did everything become so dang complicated? I'll be the first to admit the trap is real. Pick up a magazine, look on Instagram, visit a specialty store, and the message is everywhere: *You need this new piece of equipment.* If you're running a marathon, you must have this or you won't finish. We see a shiny photo of a pro athlete wearing certain gear or endorsing a product, and it has to be ours! I have an "older" GPS watch that works fine, but there's a new one out, and it has a couple of extra features that mine doesn't have.

Slow down. Strip down.

Years and years ago, when I was a classroom teacher, I worked at a running shoe store on the weekends and in the summer. It was a great side job at the time—lots of athletically-minded people on staff and frequenting the store—so I was in heaven. New products poured in, promising a faster time and better recovery, and all the reps gave us free samples to try.

But I was rarely impressed. After working there for about eight years, the cycle was clear. New products would come in, but they'd rarely last.

Do you know what lasts?

Setting goals. Hard work. Creating discipline in your life so you can achieve those goals.

When I run, I just run. No music, no GPS watch, just a pair of shoes and me. There's so much noise in our lives already, so why complicate things even more when you're focused on a workout. This holds true even more for people who are beginning. Just start running.

Don't worry about what kind of shirt you should wear. Sometimes I wear a cotton shirt, just to mix it up (and appreciate my technical running shirts that much more).

Don't worry about compression socks or even what brand of sock you should be wearing. Just go outside and move.

Don't worry about what type of gels you should buy based on amino acid balance in relation to protein. Just grab something to eat and go.

What matters most is eating right and preparing your body for the run. You can have all the latest gear with bells and whistles, but if you aren't putting the right fuel in your body to perform, it's not going to matter how far you run or what you're wearing.

You'll figure it out as you go.

The Flintstones was one of my favorite cartoons. One thing about the show that always stuck with me was how simply they lived. I mean, they did live in the Stone Age, but it was simple. They didn't even wear shoes.

When you get caught up with all the bling of running, you quickly lose sight of why you're actually out there. We need more "Barney style" (as in, Barney Rubble) in our lives. I mean they ran in bare feet; how much simpler can you get?!

I challenge you to simplify—your routine, what you wear, how you prepare, what you bring along—and see what happens.

Ideas to Consider and Share

What can you leave at home for your next workout? See what happens and how it impacts the time spent outside.

Share your stories on Instagram, Facebook, Twitter, and Strava.

#RUNLAP

GIVE YOURSELF CREDIT FOR
WHAT YOU'VE ALREADY DONE.
THERE'S ALWAYS MORE TO
DO, BUT ACKNOWLEDGING
PROGRESS IS IMPORTANT
AND KEEPS YOU MOTIVATED.

Chapter Seventeen

FEAR AND EXCUSES

It's either fear or an excuse.
Neither are good.

Haven't started running because you're busy at work? Excuse. Friends invited you to run a local 5K but you're "not available that day"? Fear.

Went to bed too late last night and hit the snooze button on your alarm? Excuse.

Out of shape and don't want to be seen running? Fear.

Fear and excuses are debilitating. They cut you off at the knees and won't allow you to make any type of progress. The antidote is to make running an integrated part of your life—not just something you do when you have time or feel good.

Family, sleeping, reading, eating, work, running. Non-negotiable.

Everything else is optional. No more excuses and forget about your fear.

#RunLAP Reflections from Jessica Cabeen

Principal, Minnesota, @JessicaCabeen

"And now that you don't have to be
perfect, you can be good."
—John Steinbeck

Saturday, July 15, 2017. The day I completed my first full 5K (3.1 miles) without stopping since my knee injury in March was also the day I signed up for the California International Marathon.

My last marathon was in 2003, and my life looked completely different. I had been married for a year, and my incredible husband was working seventy hours a week. I was a music therapist by day and a college student by night, taking courses for my teaching license and special education degree. I had room in my life for eight-mile training runs during the week and twenty-mile runs on the weekends, leading up to my first—and possibly last—marathon.

Now it's 2017. I still have that incredible husband (who took a different job so he could spend more time with his family) plus two boys, a dog, and an incredible calling as an elementary school principal. So why in the world would I want to add more to the plate? And if adding more, why a marathon?

A second marathon was a bucket list item. My first was so long ago that I started to think there was a statute of limitations for claiming it. I had seen so many possible marathons come and go, but the list of excuses I made for missing them continued to grow. Doubt, fear, and worry were the feelings that held me back from my dreams, and then guilt set in from not trying.

I have been so consumed with fear about all the reasons I might not train enough, be fast enough, or finish that I forgot the reasons I wanted to finish another marathon: because I said I would.

How many times do we challenge, encourage, and support our students to do something they don't think they can accomplish? As a parent, aunt, uncle, or family friend, have you ever supported a child to reach for their dreams—no matter how high? I came to a realization that if I expect others to reach for their dreams, I needed to stop covering mine with black clouds of doubt and just try.

Tuesday, August 1, 2017 (the day I wrote this for Adam), is the first day of my eighteen-week marathon training plan. I can't tell you the end of this story or if I finish the marathon. But I now realize the happy ending isn't about *finishing* the marathon. It's about *starting*. Because today is the day I stop wondering, worrying, and wishing I would have run that marathon.

Today is the day I start trying.

Ideas to Consider and Share

What excuses are you making that keep you from getting up and going outside? How can you squash those excuses and fear to move forward?

Share your stories on Instagram, Facebook, Twitter, and Strava.

 #RUNLAP

YOU HAVE ONE AT BAT,
ONE CHANCE, ONE TIME,
ONE LIFE—IF YOU'RE
BREATHING, YOU CAN DO
IT. YOU CAN KEEP GOING;
NOW GO.

Chapter Eighteen

I Thought I Was

You always get a second chance.
It's called tomorrow.

hree weeks of rest between marathons isn't much, but that's exactly how much time I had after my not-so-stellar April performance and heading into the Santa Cruz marathon in May.

One of the unintended benefits of running a marathon every month for a year is that you can try it again in a very short period of time. Didn't eat right? Try again next month. Didn't hydrate enough? Drink more next month. Didn't have enough long runs? You have three weeks to make a change.

Quite a few family and friends asked if I was worried about the next marathon because the last two were tough. Some asked if I thought about cancelling my running goal for the year.

Never!

Looking back has some importance. You can learn from mistakes and make adjustments. But looking forward is the only option for growth. Learn from the past, but look ahead to get your mind in a positive place to perform.

That's exactly what I did in the three weeks running up to this next race. Santa Cruz was an easy choice because it's not too far from our house, we have family in town to stay with, the course is along the ocean, and it's a smaller race, which I like.

Recovery and training went well in those twenty-one days. I was still eating a vegan diet and feeling strong. I'd been helping coach a Hero Boys running team at one of the elementary schools in our district, which is basically like Girls on the Run, but for boys. Our group was awesome. They'd progressed from barely being able to run a lap and complaining all the time to ready for their 5K race—the day before my marathon.

The problem was that the 5K was in San Francisco at Crissy Field. I almost didn't go because I had to get down to Santa Cruz, pick up my bib at the expo, and then hightail it to our family member's house, where they were hosting a barbecue for us.

I couldn't bail on the kids. It didn't feel right because they wanted me there. It was absolutely magical to see those boys in their matching shirts, getting ready to run, and in awe of the crowd.

The 5K went very well. Some kids were in serious oxygen deficit, but everyone finished and had a great time. I sprinted to my car, so I could make the marathon expo and have some time to relax before the race.

Santa Cruz is a popular spot and there's really only one way in—a curvy highway with just two lanes going each way. Most Saturdays, when the weather is nice, it can take a couple of hours in the car. As I was driving, checking the clock, trying to entertain the kids, talk with my wife, figure out what I'm eating for dinner, and looking at the map to find the expo, my wife had an idea.

"Can you drop us off at the cousins' house first, so the kids can play and swim? Then you can go to the race expo."

"But your aunt's house is past the expo. Let's just hit the expo first and then go to her house."

You know whose idea won. And of course, it was the right thing to do for the family. We drove past the expo, to the house, unloaded everything, and I drove another twenty minutes back to the expo. I was frustrated to say the least and just wanted to relax. But the expo was kind of a fiasco. Parking wasn't great, and I had to walk almost two miles each way to grab my bib and race shirt.

By this point of the day, it was almost time to eat dinner, and I'd been going nonstop all day. Up at 5 a.m., drove to San Francisco, ran a 5K with a bunch of elementary boys, sat in traffic for a couple hours, and zoomed through the race expo. I needed to eat and get ready to race.

Life is fun, but it's also complicated. In running twelve marathons in one year, working full time, being married, having two children and a dog, speaking, writing this book, and everything else that comes up in life, I'm used to managing lots of moving parts. You can plan all you want, yet things come up that are completely out of your control. For this reason alone, it's so important to keep your training varied—because life is varied.

After an amazing dinner, I was in bed by 8:30 p.m. Thankfully, our aunt's house was only a four-minute walk to the start of the race. I felt extremely mellow about this race. After my last two marathons and all the running around the day before, my goal was to have fun, smile, and finish classy.

Santa Cruz, like many marathons, had a half-marathon as well. But in this case, the half started at the same time as the full. For me, this was a problem. When I see people running faster than me, I want to catch them.

And this is why discipline and training is the most important factor when running marathons. Run your own race, period.

The race started, and the pace was fast. *Run your own race; keep your own pace, Adam.*

And I did. My pace started to pick up because I felt amazing. When the horde of half-marathoners pushed their pace, I slowed down. We ran along the ocean with a bunch of roller hills, and I made sure to control my breathing. I focused on hydration and nutrition—and finished the first 13.1 miles feeling awesome and with a great time.

The second half went along the coast in the opposite direction, so other runners were few and far between. The past twenty-four hours were a whirlwind, and I thought I was in for a repeat performance of pain and anguish—slogging through another marathon while trying to accomplish this (seemingly insane) running goal.

But the crash never happened. I ran my own race. At Mile 20, when my body still felt amazing, I just kept on running. I ate. I chatted with other runners. We ran beside spectacular bluffs just a few feet from the ocean below.

One foot in front of the other, thousands and thousands of times.

As I approached Mile 25, I almost started to sprint. I was on the verge of breaking 3:40 for this marathon, and for a few strides, I thought that would help redeem my previous races. Maybe I should have sprinted, but my discipline kept me in check, and I continued my own race. Crossing the line in 3:42 with my family cheering was the best feeling in a long time. I'd run my own race, focused on my body, and kept my mind clear, even with all the antics of the previous day.

When you think you don't have it in you or you've experienced recent failures, always go back to your training and the discipline you've built up. Trust in that, run your own race, and always remember to smile!

Ideas to Consider and Share

When is a time you've been surprised by your performance? Did you think you weren't ready or just weren't going to perform well?

Share your stories on Instagram, Facebook, Twitter, and Strava.

#RUNLAP

SACRIFICE IS ALL PART
OF THE GAME. THERE ARE
THINGS YOU'LL STOP DOING
AND NEW THINGS YOU'LL
START. IF YOU WANT IT BAD
ENOUGH, YOU'RE GONNA
NEED TO SACRIFICE.

Chapter Nineteen

JUGGLING ACT

If you want it bad enough, you'll be creative enough to find a way!

As a family of racers, you name it, we've probably done it. Jogging stroller on the top of our car, driving across two states so we could run when we got there? Check.

Kids riding their scooters or bikes in the school parking lot so I can run laps around the track? Check.

Going to bed at 9:00 p.m. and waking up at midnight when my wife got home from work so I can run ten miles? Check.

Bringing gear with me to work, changing in my car during lunch, and getting a quick run in? Cooling off and putting my work outfit back on so I can join a meeting? Check and check.

Running eight miles on the morning of my wedding day? Nope. Just kidding—check.

Waking up at 2:00 a.m. so I can get a run in before a 7:00 a.m. flight across the country? Check.

Life is a juggling act, and you have to be creative in your quest for a healthy you.

#RunLAP Reflections from David Hoffert

Superintendent, Indiana, @dahoffert

My love for running started as an awkward, shy, and uncon-fident freshman in high school . . . until one day when a teacher saw something in me that I did not see in myself. He recognized a student that, with the right encouragement, could turn into a confi-dent, all-state distance runner during the next three years.

That teacher set my course in life. At graduation, I knew I wanted to become an educator in my hometown and find the stu-dents who, like me, needed a calm and encouraging voice. I had the privilege to return to Warsaw as a history teacher and head coach for boys' track.

Life started happening and slowly cut into running. While the lessons learned never left, the actual time hitting the pavement dwindled. My competitive nature became an excuse to stay away from running. *Why should I run? I will never be as fast as I was in high school and college.* All the while, life progressed with a family, becoming a principal, PhD research, early and late meetings with fast food, and the stress of a school superintendent.

My wife watched this all transpire, until one day my medi-cal exam came back saying I was a case for a heart attack in my mid-thirties. A gift showed up at my doorstep: a new pair of run-ning shoes. I wondered if I would ever feel like a runner again. After a couple of weeks, I decided I was going to do a crash course in dis-tance running, going from no running to a full marathon in roughly two months. It hurt, and I swore I was done with running forever.

The reality was that I could not stay away. I found the solitude of running provided time for reflection. Long runs have also become a social event, with a faithful running partner (a fellow educator)—as we joke about solving all the world and educational problems one mile at a time. Running helped me find a balance that was missing in my life. It made me a better superintendent, husband, and father. Two years and nine marathons later, I find myself in the final training days for the Boston Marathon and dreaming of new goals.

Ideas to Consider and Share

Life is busy; how do you keep everything organized and still find time to accomplish what you need to happen?

Share your stories on Instagram, Facebook, Twitter, and Strava.

#RUNLAP

THE POTENTIAL IS INSIDE
OF YOU; IT'S YOUR OWN
PERSONAL POTENTIAL. YOU
MAY NOT EVEN KNOW WHAT'S
IN THERE, BUT IT'S UP TO
YOU TO GO AND FIND IT.

Chapter Twenty

LET'S TALK ABOUT VEGAN

I like eating plants; that's it.

It was probably a long time coming, and I just didn't realize it. In all honesty, if you would have asked me five years ago if I'd go from vegetarian to vegan, I'd have looked at you a little sideways.

It wasn't that big of a leap; I just needed something big to happen to make the commitment. I'd been a vegetarian for about ten years, my wife hasn't eaten meat since she was sixteen, and our kids have never had meat.

Looking back to my childhood, my mom always said I was a good eater. My dad told me later in life that it didn't matter how much food they put on my plate for dinner, I would always eat everything. I was a busy kid to say the least and needed the calories. When I played Little League baseball, my nickname was Mr. Excitement, so you get the point.

My vegan journey began even before I decided to run twelve marathons in 2017. I've always been a voracious reader, a fan of podcasts, and consume lots of information about diet, the environment, and endurance athletes who accomplish big things. I originally started eating vegetarian because of my concern for animal rights, and it quickly turned into the trifecta of animal rights, my health, and environmental reasons.

Right after I signed up for all twelve marathons in December of 2016, I pulled all the information I'd previously read about a vegan diet and endurance athletes. I normally wouldn't even consider myself an endurance athlete, but for argument's sake and the fact I was running all those marathons, I put myself into the category.

It turns out that eating dairy can cause inflammation in the joints for some people, so not eating it can boost recovery after an endurance event. I wasn't eating the animal when I consumed cheese or ice cream, but those products were still directly linked to them and, in my opinion, causing harm to the planet.

And the final kicker was the amazing podcast put out by Rich Roll. Rich is an absolutely legit endurance athlete and maintains a vegan diet while racing and training at a very intense level. The voices from the field that he's brought onto his show are what convinced me this was something I need to try.

But my family wasn't too sure.

"What are you going to eat, Dad?"

"Wait, no ice cream?"

"What are you going to make for dinner, Honey?" my wife asked. (I do the majority of the cooking for our family.)

Truth be told, eating plant-based (vegan) is not that difficult. When people ask about the most important thing I did during my marathon year, I always give credit to eating vegan. But the new level of recovery and lack of any type of joint pain in 2017 was beyond my expectations.

A plant-based diet is not for everyone, but there are enough endurance athletes, NFL players, movie stars, and normal guys like me who've found success with this lifestyle, and I have zero intention of ever going back.

Ideas to Consider and Share

What kind of food have you found that best fuels your body? Have you tried a vegan approach?

Share your stories on Instagram, Facebook, Twitter, and Strava.

#RUNLAP

WHEN IT GETS HARD, I JUST TELL MYSELF I CAN. MOST OF THE TIME THAT'S ALL IT TAKES.

Chapter Twenty-One

Day In and Day Out

I already know where I'm going tomorrow morning. I'm going for a run.

I must admit that I really don't *train*. I just go out and run. I throw a longer run in once in a while to get ready for race day and run hills on a consistent basis, but I tend to keep the activity pretty simple.

But I *run*. A lot. There's not a week that goes by where I haven't run at least five days or had some type of physical activity. Between my wife and me, there's an unspoken, *How far are you running today?* And our kids even speak this language. During the day when I call my wife to check in and see how things are, the first question is always about her run—where she went and how she felt. When I don't run, I feel like a border collie locked up in a cage.

For some people, it's hard to get in the routine; for others it's easy. I always tell people not to make running, working out, or whatever passion you have something *extra*. Make it a non-negotiable part of your day.

#RunLAP Reflections from Kas Nelson
Principal, Oklahoma, @kasnelson

I didn't run in high school. In fact I played a couple of team sports and loathed running to get in shape. Through those team sports, I also learned I wasn't gifted with speed. So how (and why?) would a slow non-runner ever consider running?

It was for a combination of reasons that I decided to give running a try almost twenty years ago. I was looking for an activity I could do practically anytime or anywhere. (We have few fitness centers here, so running appealed to me because there happens to be a lot of open road in rural Northwest Oklahoma.) Also, I had a friend who was a runner and encouraged me to try. We even began running together in the early mornings before I headed to school to teach. I look back on that time, and I am so thankful that I began running because the activity means so much more to me now. It's made me more confident and has shown me that I'm capable of much more than I'd ever imagined.

Currently, I am *runstreaking*. Streaking means that I'm committed to running at least a mile every day. I've run at 2:00 a.m., before an early morning plane, and I've run at 11:59 p.m., after a full day of leading my school and attending school functions. I've run through illness and through sorrow at the loss of those I love most. Through my streak, I've run several 5K races and two half-marathons. I've completed daily runs in Oklahoma, New Mexico, Colorado, California, Texas, Kansas, Pennsylvania, Maryland, Virginia, Missouri, Arkansas, and Louisiana. Throughout this streak, running has taught me discipline, dedication, and grit. I wrote the following poem as an expression of why I run. Enjoy!

She laces up.

Her ears listen for the beckoning road.

She's tired. Drained. Exhausted.

The day's events have taken their toll.

She's ready. Ready to take off. Ready to go.

Ready.

She sets out on today's journey.

The sun greets her, and the breeze embraces her like a long-lost friend.

Her feet keep the beat for the ensuing song.

A song made up of moments that create the melody inside her.

She breathes. In. Out. In. Out.

She pushes.

Pushes the day's events from her mind.

Pushes positive thoughts to herself.

Pushes her body, her legs, her boundaries.

She begins to feel revived. Alive.

She's lighter—the weight of the day is being expunged.

She runs because it reminds her that she can do anything she puts her mind to—she can choose to persevere.

She runs because she's a mother, and she wants to model an active lifestyle for her children.

She runs because in times of sorrow, stress, and worry, running is her comfort.

She runs because she can.

Every run is a new song. New moments. New life.

Tomorrow.

She laces up.

Ideas to Consider and Share

What type of routine do you have? Do you stick to it? If you don't, what's holding you back?

Share your stories on Instagram, Facebook, Twitter, and Strava.

#RUNLAP

Chapter Twenty-Two
LIKE SO MANY

When things don't go as planned,
chill. Everything will work out,
but you gotta chill!

raveling and racing can be a blast, especially if you can do both
with your entire family.

June brought us to Seattle and the Rock-n-Roll Marathon, which
I'd been looking forward to for a long time. For years, friends of mine
have run either a half or full with this series, and one of my neighbors
actually ran every half marathon in the series a few years back. The
anticipation had been building; it was my time now.

This was also a family weekend away, and we were going to stay
with family in Seattle. The part about dad running a marathon definitely played second fiddle. My kids were way more pumped to fly on
a plane, play with their cousin, go on a ferry, visit a new state, and get
breakfast while Dad runs.

This race was also the-marathon-before-the-halfway-mark-of-
the-year, and I was excited. At the same time, running marathons was
becoming pretty routine. I'd already run five marathons this year and

six in the last six months. I knew what needed to happen to get across the finish line, and I wasn't too worried about all we were doing in the days before. A little added bonus was that my wife's cousin was running the half and we'd travel to the start—and be able to celebrate at the finish—together.

Family time was great. We visited downtown, went to the famous fish market, kids went for a swim in the pool, we rode a ferry, had tofu tacos, and had an awesome time with family. Now it was time to run.

On paper, Seattle Rock-n-Roll was a pretty moderate course. Yes, there were a few hills, and you never know the weather up north, but there weren't any huge concerns that jumped out in my pre-race recon. Very rarely do I know a course that well the first time around. And being a fairly experienced marathoner, I also know the course maps tell one story, and the road tells the real story.

My goal was 3:45 for this race, and they had plenty of pace groups to join—which I knew would be helpful to follow as these are usually local runners who can chat about the course. As with all marathons now, the police presence at the start was everywhere. There's always music at the start of a race, but they were bumping in Seattle, loud and hard. Don't get me wrong, the music was awesome and definitely puts a smile on your face when you're getting ready to run. But I learned many years ago that I do better when I stay in my own brain with my thoughts, my plan, and my approach to this race.

The starts of races are usually hectic. Racers bump into you, try to get a better position, find a friend, or who knows what else. My philosophy is, *we have a long way to run—remember to chill.*

Off we went. The course was beautiful, as we ran around Lake Seattle and through many different neighborhoods. I felt strong and relaxed, nutrition and hydration were on point, I saw my wife and kids at Mile 10 (which is always a boost to morale) and for all intents and purposes was on cruise control.

As predicted, the pacers were legit. Two local runners knew the course really well and were great to chat with about running and pretty much anything anyone wanted to talk about. What I didn't know was these were the "first" pacers. They were only going to run with us for 13.1 miles, and then two "fresh" pacers were going to pick up the group. I've never seen this before, and their explanation was they wanted to ensure people met their goals, and the fresh runners would take us across the line. *Okay, sounds good!*

And then we picked up the new pacers.

To be completely fair, everyone running a marathon is running their own marathon. I believe that and take responsibility for how I train, how I approach race day, and what happens on the course. But when we picked up the fresh pacers, who probably slept longer than us the night before and hadn't already run a half marathon, things were about to get interesting. The handoff went without any issue, and then they turned up the pace. My heart rate increased, I couldn't have casual conversation as easily, and my GPS watch pleaded, "Yo, Adam, what's going on with the pace?"

We hit the first hill with our new pacers, and the group fell apart. People fell off the pace, some tried to sprint and catch up, others started to walk, and I went back to my training. *Run your own race, forget the pacers, don't worry about the group, drink some water, have some food, put a smile on your face, one foot in front of the other, and finish this race.* That short, but intense, burst didn't put too much hurt on me, but I definitely wasn't the same and spent a few miles recovering.

At Mile 18, we ran right by the finish—a huge stadium where the Seattle Seahawks' football team plays and where all the half-marathoners finished with smiles on their faces. And we still have eight more miles to go. If you've never run a marathon before, eight miles might sound like nothing. *You've already run this far; how hard could another eight be?*

And this is where the course map doesn't tell the whole story.

On paper there was an easy out and back along the highway to finish the race. The views of the city and harbor were amazing. But I wasn't looking at either because a headwind was rocking me in the face, and the ever-so-slight uphill (which seemed like uphill both ways) was the hidden trap of the course. And then it started to rain.

Bring it on.

Each and every time I face a struggle, it makes me stronger and more capable the next time I face a challenge. This race was supposed to be like so many other ones, and it most definitely was not—which is what I love about marathons. The amount of variables are beyond measure. Training at the same time every day, with the same factors you always deal with, will give you those same exact results. But it will not prepare you for when things go sideways.

I finished the race in 4:06, which was disappointing indeed. But I'm always reminded, it's not about the time. It's about what you learned. It's about the people you meet, the adventures that happen, and the way you feel after processing the experience. Seattle was supposed to be like so many other marathons, and without knowing it, it was something very special that I think about to this day.

Ideas to Consider and Share

When is a time you went out unprepared and had to navigate on the fly? What did you learn? What would you change in your training to get better prepared for next time?

Share your stories on Instagram, Facebook, Twitter, and Strava.

#RUNLAP

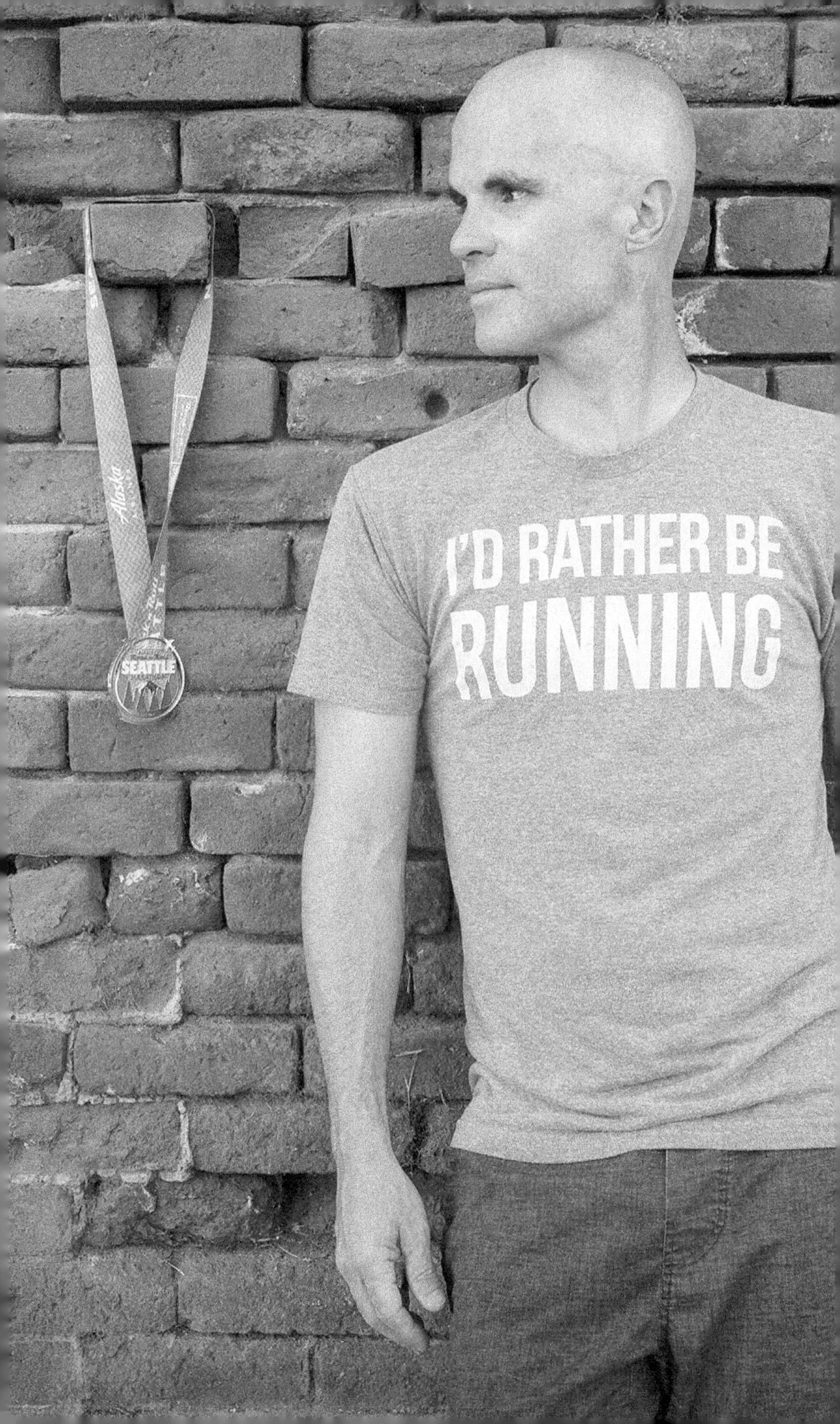
I'D RATHER BE
RUNNING
SEATTLE
Alaska

LOOK AHEAD, BUT ALWAYS
FOCUS ON THE CHALLENGE
THAT IS DIRECTLY IN
FRONT OF YOU.

Chapter Twenty-Three

DAD, WHY AREN'T YOU TALKING?

Pushing one hundred pounds while you run is amazing . . . training.

*P*ushing the jogging stroller was a time in my life I'll never forget. My wife and I were brand new parents, and getting our daughter outside in the fresh air and exposing her to an active lifestyle was of utmost importance. Eventually we didn't have to put Greta in the (heavy) car seat attachment.

And then our son was born. I can remember being at the store with the kids, carrying Tilden in the front pack and keeping close tabs on Greta because she loved to run around the store and away from us. My wife was at work, and I wasn't even mission-shopping for it, but there it was. It was huge. I wasn't even sure if it would fit in our car, but I knew we needed it. And it was on sale. So what did I do? I asked the kids!

"Do you think we should buy that double jogging stroller, so mom and dad can push you both on our runs?"

"Yes, Daddy!"

Our first jogging stroller was blue, which we always liked, but this one was yellow and had the Ironman logo on the side. Sweet! I really wanted to surprise my wife when she got home from work. So we kept it in the box and strapped it to the top of my car.

Of course, the first thing we did when we got home was put the wheels on and go for a run! Oh, my gosh, was it awesome. And oh, my gosh, it was huge—like, *you can't push this doublewide stroller on the sidewalk without people having to get out of the way* kind of huge.

The day we brought it home, we had the talk.

"Honey, let's go run that half marathon again where that guy yelled at me last year! Maybe he'll be out there again, and I can pass him while pushing this beast!"

That was the beginning of thousands of miles, a few Turkey Trots, and a handful of half marathons with The Beast.

A few years later, something happened which has stuck with me to this day. I was ramping up training for an upcoming marathon, and I needed to get a fifteen miler in with some rolling hills. One of our favorite places to run in my hometown is a beautiful multi-use trail. A hundred years ago, it was the old railroad tracks that went through town. Those trains are long gone, and now it's a great place to run and ride bikes. My wife and I usually had a deal worked out: she would run with the dog, and I would push the jogging stroller.

Some people may think I was trying to show some chivalry to my wife, but I'll let you in on a little secret. Pushing that double stroller, which weighed close to one-hundred pounds, was amazing training. There are still times when I wish we had that stroller, and I could push it for the resistance it provided for so many years.

It was time for the fifteen-mile training. We were warmed up and throwing down a nice eight-minute pace on the way out. At Mile 7, there's a pretty steep hill, which lasts for a half mile before it flattens out and we turn around to go back down. We're running, I'm pushing, kids are talking, and the hill is coming. I sip some water, the hill is here, and then my son started. Both of my kids have amazing personalities and can carry a conversation with anyone, even adults. But he is the question asker of the two.

"Hey Dad. When we get home, I want to build a big fort in the living room with blankets and chairs; maybe we could make some lasers, too, and have a battle against the girls. Then, if we get hungry, how about we make sandwiches and have a little campout in the fort!"

"Dad."

"Daddy."

"Dad, why aren't you talking?"

His voice was a little bit strained, and I could tell he was getting nervous because I wasn't responding. Of course, he knew I was still there because we were going up a half-mile-long hill, and who did he think was pushing him and his sister? So he got louder.

"DAD, WHY AREN'T YOU TALKING?!"

"Hey, buddy. I can't. Talk right now. I'm pushing."

We got to the top of the hill, had some water, and I tried to explain my silence. Did the kids get it? Probably not. Does it matter? Not at all. My wife and I still laugh about that run, and it wasn't the last time either of them asked us if we were still back there.

We never did see that guy again on the half marathon course, but it didn't really matter. We knew what it took to push a single jogger, let alone a double. It would have been fun to pass him again, pushing the wide load—even if I couldn't speak!

Ideas to Consider and Share

Do you have any funny stories from your kids or friends on a workout?

Share your stories on Instagram, Facebook, Twitter, and Strava.

Chapter Twenty-Four

My Body

My body is important; only good things go in.

How you feel is a direct reflection of what you put into your body. If you take care of your body, it will take care of you when you need it to. The stakes were definitely higher than usual in 2017, but the way I treated my body was no different than usual.

Do I drink alcohol? Very little. I've realized the more I train and the better I eat, the more focus I have and the better I feel when I don't drink. Alcohol has lots of calories, dehydrates you, and can take your focus away from what matters most.

I eat organic. Is it more expensive? In most cases, it is. But I'm never sick. The food tastes better too. Try eating an apple after you've taken all extra sugar out of your diet. That fruit tastes like nothing you've ever eaten before. It's fresh, crisp, has an abundance of flavor, and it'll make you feel better while you're training.

Do I stretch? Not enough. I've read so many conflicting studies and research articles over the years about stretching. So I developed my own plan that works for me. I like to roll. My two favorite methods are the stick rollers and a big foam roller for my legs and other muscles when they need it. Just because there's an article in some magazine that gives you advice doesn't mean you need to mirror what they suggest. Everybody has a different body, a different agenda, and needs something different to get them from the starting line to the finish.

When in doubt, take care of your body. Analyze what you eat, how you train, how much you sleep, how much sitting you do during the day, when you train, why you train, how you train, and who you train with. Your body is important; take care of it.

Ideas to Consider and Share

What are your favorite foods to eat when training? Do you have any favorite stretches or ways you loosen up your muscles? Any other tips or tricks to share?

Share your stories on Instagram, Facebook, Twitter, and Strava.
#*RUNLAP*

Chapter Twenty-Five

I Can't Help Myself

If you're gonna do it, really do it!

Lots of people talk about having balance in their lives. They focus on their family, not working too much, taking time for self-care, and maybe you could say they live a calm and relaxed life.

For me, balance is out the window. I focus on being fanatical. In high school it was baseball, in college I snowboarded, and in my twenties, it was cycling. I used to ride my bike twenty miles each way to work, five days a week, for seven years. And on the weekend, there was always a ninety miler some day and a fifty or sixty the other day.

Family and kids came along, and cycling was too time-intensive to be viable. That's why I run.

Running marathons helps me analyze every aspect of my life, to gain better performance and to feel stronger on race day.

I wear each pair of running shoes for a month. Some people (I won't mention any names) think the shoes still have plenty of life in them. What I know, however, is that *I've never been injured, and running in fresh shoes is a good thing!* On the twentieth of each month, I start choosing my next pair. Which one should be next? What color scheme have I not worn in a while? It's always the same shoe: the Brooks Adrenalines have been the faithful choice for many years, but I'm always thinking about the next pair.

Each day I flash forward. *Is anything I'm eating right now going to negatively affect my run tomorrow morning?* Just because I eat vegan doesn't mean I have a free pass. Too much fruit can give me a stomachache—not enough calories and I'll bonk. I'm running tomorrow morning. I just can't help myself.

Ideas to Consider and Share

What are you fanatical about? Have you tried incorporating more balance into your life?

Share your stories on Instagram, Facebook, Twitter, and Strava.

#RUNLAP

Chapter Twenty-Six

LIKE SO MANY THINGS

People look at the end and get all
excited. I look at the work it takes to
get to the end. That gets me excited.

*T*he more experiences I have, the more marathons I run, the
more people I talk with, the more struggles I endure, the more
struggles I see other people endure, I've come to realize something.
Training, preparing for, and running a marathon is like many other
things in life.

We live in a culture with so much focus on the finish line—and
the selfie holding the medal, smiling ear to ear in celebration.

Life isn't a sprint; it's a marathon. A sprint is quick. You can see
the finish line from the start. A marathon makes you put in the work.
A marathon takes you places you've never been before. A marathon
can put you in the "pain cave" even on your best days. A marathon
makes you slow down; it makes you do what needs to be done so you
actually do cross that finish line. A marathon keeps it real.

And to me, that's life.

Life isn't a hack that will get you to the front of the line. Life isn't one lap around the track, and you're done. Life isn't all play with no work.

So much of what we do is ninety-five percent work and five percent celebration. When I start a marathon, I've already done ninety-five percent of the work. Running the race and crossing the finish line only encompasses five percent of the overall work. Races are completed because of the work you put in when nobody's looking.

The grind. The grit. The struggle. The failure. The planning. The pain. The training.

That's what I want people to see because it's like so many things in life.

As educators, this conversation is more important than ever. A school year is a marathon, and you must pace yourself. If you take off on a sprint the first two weeks of the year, you're going to burn out. Pace yourself. Show kids that you're playing the long game. The short game will get you paid now, but we're playing the long game for that bigger payout at the end of the year—next year—and in five years.

I fully realize not everyone wants to, or even can, run a marathon. But what you can do is something requiring preparation, planning, and dedication—going farther than you ever have, faster than you thought was possible, more days in a row than you think you have time for.

Running a marathon is just like so many things in life. Put in the work. Keep your eye on the prize. Stay focused. Be humble. Take care of your body and mind. And cross that finish line when the time comes.

Ideas to Consider and Share

Are you sprinting or preparing for the marathon? How are you preparing for the long game and not just focusing on the short game with quick dividends?

Share your stories on Instagram, Facebook, Twitter, and Strava.

#RUNLAP

STOP TALKING ABOUT WHAT YOU WANT TO DO AND START DOING WHAT YOU WANT TO DO. IF YOU DON'T, IT'S JUST NOT GOING TO HAPPEN.

Chapter Twenty-Seven

GOALS

If you don't set a goal, you have nothing to chase.

How many times have you set a goal and not achieved it? How many people have goals but never do anything to make them happen? Have you written out a goal on your computer or a piece of paper, and it's still just sitting there? How often do you not set goals when you could?

Running marathons reminds me I can do difficult things, over and over and over again!

The first step with goal setting is to think big. I've always tried to think really big, and take small actions on a daily basis. Your goals should be a stretch, but also attainable at an "I'm not sure I'm going to achieve this" level. For example, if you're trying to up your running game and you've been running 5K races once a month, don't just settle for a 10K. It's time to stretch what you've done and go after a half-marathon. Without a doubt, you'll push yourself to train and run 13.1 miles, but if you don't push, you may never know what you're capable of. It's time for a new goal.

When you set a goal, commit and make it all public. Find some accountability partners to help get you through.

In December of 2016, the "marathon year" idea got me totally excited. And then, a few minutes later, a sense of "uh oh" came over me. *Could I run that many marathons in one year? Would my body hold up under all those miles? Would I be able to balance work and family life? What if I couldn't finish all the races? Would eating vegan give me the calories I needed and help me to recover quickly?*

That "uh oh" feeling was exactly what I was after. It was uncertain. It was a stretch. It was new and big. I knew well enough that there would be some challenging times for an entire year.

Struggle adds value, it helps build hope, it brings you through the fray and to the other side with another layer of armor—which helps protect you against future uncertainty and hard times. When you struggle and dig deep to achieve your goals, you build strength in areas you didn't have before. You become brave against the enemies that hibernate in your body and try to expose your weaknesses.

Those weaknesses disguise themselves as your friends.

They tell you it's okay to stop and take a rest. They tell you to hit the snooze button and sleep in; "You can always train tomorrow." They tell you to eat more dessert or have another drink because you had a rough week at work.

Don't listen to them.

When you're committed, your goals have a stronger voice. They don't listen to the enemies in your body trying to derail your success. Don't get me wrong; what you want to achieve looks hard. You can feel how hard it is. But stop and take another look. You'll see what all the hype is about and want to charge up that hill to achieve the greatness you so rightfully deserve.

Forget small; think big! Act big, push yourself, crush those enemies, and go make something amazing happen.

#RunLAP Reflections from Brandi Miller
First Grade Teacher, Florida, @bmilla84

Growing up, I always struggled with my self-image. As a young adult, I did not choose healthy habits. As I approached the big 3-0, I decided to make a lifestyle change. I began walking with my best friend, Nicole, and was perfectly content staying in my neighborhood, where no one could see me. Every time Nicole would push me to run, I'd tell her, "I'm not a runner!"

A year later, I decided to run the Walt Disney World Half Marathon with my best friends, Nicole and Jen. I had never dreamed of doing something like that, but I wanted a big goal to work towards. So the three of us agreed to sign up, train, and run the race together.

Training began and as the mileage increased, I had doubts and struggles. Some days the run was easy and, other days, dreadful. In my mind, I still wasn't a runner. However, Nicole continually reinforced that I *was* a runner because I was out there moving! I had to learn that running was more mental than it was physical. I could push my body to do more than I thought I could.

On the day of the half-marathon, the three of us raced together the entire way and stuck to our training plan. The first nine miles were exciting, energetic, and more then I imagined. However, as we approached Mile 10, I was ready to quit. My body was tired, my mind was doubtful, and I was ready to stop. Mile 10 was the on-ramp heading back towards Epcot, and everyone was slowing down and walking up the ramp.

Nicole and Jen encouraged me to finish strong. Through the tears, I took those moments of walking to regroup and set my sights on finishing the race.

More tears flowed as I crossed the finish line. I had never dreamed of completing a half marathon, let alone with my best friends by my side. In life sometimes you need to slow down in order to finish the race strong. I proved to myself that I was a runner! I learned it's not about being the fastest or the best but believing in yourself and never giving up.

Ideas to Consider and Share

What are your goals and what are you doing to help make them happen?

Share your stories on Instagram, Facebook, Twitter, and Strava.

#RUNLAP

Chapter Twenty-Eight

THE GOLDEN GATE

Running across the Golden Gate Bridge is special anytime you can do it.

Hometown races are always special. You can sleep in your own bed the night before. The course is usually more familiar. Family can easily come to hang out and cheer you on, and there's not as much running around without all the travel of destination races.

But the San Francisco marathon was also the *over the halfway mark* for my marathon year. This running project of mine was coming along nicely, and I'd definitely found my groove with training and preparation. When you're in the moment, it can be difficult to step away and reflect on what's already been accomplished. I'd run six marathons in six months that year, and my body was feeling amazing. By this point, I'd also decided to add a couple of additional races to the calendar in December.

Look ahead, but always focus on the challenge that is directly in front of you.

This one wasn't going to be easy. The one thing I had come to realize was: *don't get comfortable.* San Francisco has lots of hills, weather can always be a factor, I was coming off just two weeks of rest from the previous race, and this marathon had a 5:30 a.m. start time. We were also headed on a two-week family vacation right after the race, which took plenty of planning and preparation as well.

Parking in the city is never that great, so on race morning, I hopped on a bus to the start and enjoyed the warm weather as we waited around for things to get under way. The course for this race is pretty spectacular. It starts directly in front of the Ferry Building and goes along the Embarcadero, past Pier 39, past Crissy Field, over and back across the Golden Gate Bridge, through Golden Gate Park, and then back around the city past AT&T Park (where the San Francisco Giants play) and finally finishes back downtown.

At some races, the vibe can be pretty chill, but not San Francisco. Music was playing at the start, people were in a good mood, there was a half-marathon starting with us, and some people had run a marathon the night before and were getting ready to start their second one.

In the first few miles, I definitely had to find my groove and warm up. I wasn't worried about how I felt, but I didn't have my normal fluidity. I tried to shake it off and enjoy the course. Running past Crissy Field was fun—especially since I'd just registered for my last race of the year, which would take place there on New Year's Eve (more about that race at the end of the book).

We had our first major climb running up to the Golden Gate—a pretty sharp hill that doesn't want to stop. I love these early hills because all the runners get really quiet as they conserve energy, and racers size everyone up. I'd love to tell you that running over the bridge was amazing, and I took some awesome photos that I posted on social media. But I can't because it was so fogged in you couldn't even see the large pillars on the bridge. The fog was so thick it felt like rain, and we were all dripping wet. Thankfully, the race organizers had rubber mats covering all the steel plates that hold the bridge together, otherwise the bridge would have been quite slippery.

My time goal is always about the same; I shoot for a 3:45, which some may say is too slow for me, but I was running twelve marathons this year. Being an age group runner is completely fine with me, and 3:45 pushes me and allows me to recover quickly. I've never been injured with twenty marathons under my belt, and I like that formula!

As we approached Golden Gate Park at Mile 13, it started to get busy. Yep, all the people running the half marathon were pouring it on to finish strong. As I always say, run your race and focus on your rhythm with your pace and your goals.

I tried, but it was hard. Our pace group (3:45) stayed together pretty well, but the half-marathon traffic jam threw a wrench in the works. We were bobbing and weaving amongst the herd of runners. Up until this point, we were on pace for a 3:43 marathon, which is right where you want to be at this stage of the game. Coming out of Golden Gate Park, there's a hill, and that's where I lost the group. I was still very much in the group, but they were pulling ahead of me.

Don't stress, don't panic, stay chill, and run your race. Being with a pace group definitely builds camaraderie with the other runners, and then when you're suddenly dropped, your mindset takes a direct hit, and I always need a mental recharge when this happens. Take a sip of water, slow down my cadence, take inventory of how I'm feeling, smile, and continue on.

DON'T STRESS, DON'T PANIC, STAY CHILL, AND RUN YOUR RACE.

Golden Gate Park is absolutely beautiful; and the farther we got from the second half-marathon start, the more it loosened up—all the runners had more breathing room on the road. Yep, all the people running the half marathon were pouring it on to finish strong, and right after they finished, a second half marathon was starting. I wish I could say the 3:45 pace group slowed down and waited for me, but that's not a reality in a big marathon like San Francisco. I charged on with my own thoughts and goals. Remembering my early mantra, *don't get comfortable*, is helpful when so much is unpredictable and flexibility is key.

Coming down the final miles along the water, we ran by the new stadium, where the Golden State Warriors will play their games, and finally around AT&T Park and the home stretch. My family called out with only a couple hundred feet to go, and I stopped on the side for a kiss from everyone before crossing the line. My wife still hated it when I stopped because it hurts my time, but having my most important cheering section at this race, and any race for that matter, always means so much.

Finishing this one in 3:55 felt amazing. Was I disappointed with my time? Not at all. I'd run across a bridge, around a city, and I had just passed the halfway mark with my 2017 running goal. I couldn't have felt better or been happier.

#RunLAP Reflections from Laura Jennaro
Principal, Wisconsin, @Laura_Jennaro

Running has become an essential part of my day, a habit that allows me to start every day on the "right foot."

I love my early morning runs that I affectionately refer to as "zero dark thirty." There is something glorious about waking up and getting after it before most people start their day. I truly enjoy this solitary time. Time to contemplate; time to ruminate; time to clear my head; time to reflect. Time to push myself; time to get stronger; time to improve. A time for solitude.

I also use this time to learn, whether listening to a podcast, audiobook, or Voxer conversations. Running provides a space for whatever I need at that very moment—and without it, I notice I am not as focused or productive during my day.

I run to be strong and healthy. I love the time I have with my kids, and I want to be able to keep up with them! I run, so I can play that pick-up soccer, basketball, or gaga ball game. I also have a family history of heart disease and high cholesterol, and running helps me keep those potentially limiting issues in check.

Following a training plan keeps me focused on becoming stronger and faster, as do the races I enter. Training plans have supported this habit and kept me injury free for many years. I don't run to win races, but I compete because it keeps me honest and reminds me of the many other people out there getting after it. There is a sense of camaraderie among race participants, and the energy is unparalleled. It also provides a positive example for my kids! I am hoping to have them join me for a 5K someday soon!

Running provides a time and space for me to focus on my goals. Completing a run and logging the workout is such a wonderful feeling of accomplishment. I see progress through my logged workouts, so even if today's workout was hard and I was certain I was slower, I often find that it was faster than my previous time. That is encouragement for the next day's run, and for me there isn't a more positive way to start my day.

Why do you run?

Ideas to Consider and Share

Why do you run? Tell us. Show us. We want to hear!

Share your stories on Instagram,
Facebook, Twitter, and Strava.
#RUNLAP

SOMETIMES YOU NEED TO PUT A RALLY CAP ON TO GET YOU THROUGH. WHATEVER IT TAKES, JUST GET TO THE FINISH.

Chapter Twenty-Nine

MY IMAGINARY FRIENDS

It's okay to brag, if you've earned it.

You've gotta find your groove!

Each morning the patter of my feet, my shoes on the road, helps to find my beat. Hearing the sounds that only happen early in the morning is a privilege; most people don't hear these sounds.

My alarm goes off at 4:00 each morning. I love that time of day the most. Family is still asleep, kids aren't running around the house yet. I eat my oatmeal in solitude, and I'm out the door.

There is that daily, pivotal moment: staying in bed or getting up to run. Don't for a minute think it's an easy decision each morning. The trick for me has always been to flash forward, picturing the open road as my body warms up and thanks itself for the exercise.

Then once the morning oatmeal ritual is complete, it's out the door. My optimal time to leave the house is 4:30 a.m. because I know my kids will probably be up by 6:00 a.m., and I love to be home when they roll into the kitchen for that morning hug.

"Dad, you're all sweaty."

"How was your run?" asks my five-year-old.

"Where'd you go?"

They love knowing my route, what I saw, how I felt; these are the morning conversations we have in our house.

Those first strides down the road include checking your body for any issues, planning your route, checking for weather, tying your shoes, and making sure the dog leash isn't tangled and the Garmin watch is on; let's go!

The road each morning is so peaceful: the sounds, smells, darkness, silence, the solitude. Now comes that moment of truth; there's something I must admit.

I have a secret. My imaginary friends are always with me to help me along!

I'm serious. They're always there as I run with my headlamp on around the streets of my hometown. If it's a quick six miles or something a little longer, the motivation to push and exert comes from my friends.

A friend is ahead of us; gotta push the pace to the stop light. Let's go.

Check your six; two friends are behind and closing the gap.

Sure, my dog, Bear, is with me, but that's never enough. I need those friends in front and those trying to chase me down. My friends are my coaches. Some people use Nike+ or Strava; I have imaginary friends.

Bragging rights have always been another motivator for the early morning sessions. When you're done with a workout by 6:00 a.m., you've already had the pain, had the sweat, earned your breakfast, and feel amazing from the workout. That is what I love.

Lace up those shoes, get out the door, run with your "friends," and kick off each day with a sweat.

Ideas to Consider and Share

What keeps you going when you work out or do what you love? What's your motivation on a daily basis?

Share your stories on Instagram, Facebook, Twitter, and Strava.

#RUNLAP

NOBODY WANTS TO HEAR YOUR HACK OR SHORTCUT. THEY DON'T WORK. THE ONLY THING THAT DOES IS HARD WORK. NO SHORTCUTS, NO HACKS, NO COUPONS, NO DAYS OFF, JUST HARD WORK.

Chapter Thirty

WHEN

It doesn't take much. I pretty
much always want to go.

When I'm stressed, I run.

When I'm tired, I run.

When I need to clear my head, I run.

When I'm confused about a decision, I run.

When it's raining, I run.

When I need some alone time, I run.

When I miss my dad, I run.

When my kids are driving me nuts, I run.

When my dog needs to get out of the house, I run.

When I'm traveling, I run.

When my wife and I need some alone time, we run.

When I wake up in the middle of the night and can't sleep, I run.

When I've been on the road for a few days speaking and my legs are tight, I run.

When I need to find my inner voice that's sometimes buried deep within my body, I run.

When I'm exhausted and run down and need to flush out the toxins in my body, I run.

When I get new shoes that I'm really excited about, I run.

When I read about the world and hear about too many atrocities happening worldwide, I run.

When I know we're going out to my favorite restaurant for dinner, I run. And maybe I run a little bit further.

When I simply need to be in my thinking place and remind myself just how lucky I am to be alive, I run.

#RunLAP Reflections from Stacy Welcome

Runner, mother, wife, Emergency Department Physician Assistant, all around badass, and married to Adam!

I started running in high school and basically never stopped, with the exception of a few short hiatuses.

For me, running is like that ever-dependable friend, always there when you need him or her during the good times and the bad. Running has literally carried me through my life, including grad school in Iowa (This is where I wasn't savvy enough to run in spikes and ended up on my backside more than once from slipping on ice!), breakups, deaths, a marriage, the birth of two children, and many other significant events in between.

I started marathoning after tragically losing my best friend in a cycling accident in 2006. I challenged myself to qualify for and run in Boston in his honor and to manage my intense grief. Because running, for me, is better than any medication or therapy.

My friend/coach/running partner and I took to the streets and trails, running hills in order to prepare for "Heartbreak Hill," doing *fartleks* and speed workouts, long runs and slow runs, and even some cross training with aqua jogging and core work. When

Patriots' Day 2007 arrived, we were ready to race Boston. Despite one of the worst ever Nor'easters for a Boston Marathon and near cancellation of the race the night before due to heavy winds, we survived and finished the race with intense emotion, bruised toe-nails, and tired legs. It's amazing what one can accomplish with dedication and a strong will!

Fast forward two and a half years: still running. On a cold, December morning, when I was about to race a challenging trail half-marathon in the Marin Headlands, running brought me my destiny. I met Adam, who was also racing that day, and shortly thereafter he became my running, and life, partner. It's rather ironic to me that my love of running led me to find the love of my life!

Grief struck again in 2010, when I lost my Mom to a ten-year battle with breast cancer. Adam, family, friends, and running helped get me through it. It's always a run that brings me back to where I need to be.

Here's what I've come to realize about running:

When I'm happy, I run.

When I'm sad, I run.

When I'm stressed, I run.

When I'm angry, I run.

When I need to clear my head, I run.

When I need clarity on a difficult situation, I run.

When I want to be one with nature, I run.

When I want to be alone for some "me time," I run.

When we want to do something together as a family, we run.

Running serves many purposes in my life. It nourishes my body, spirit, and mind. It keeps me mentally and physically healthy. It helps me deal with the difficult cases I see at work in the Emergency Department/Trauma Center. It allows me to sleep well at night. But it's not always fun, and sometimes I dread getting out of bed to go run. And sometimes I feel like crap on the run, but I keep going back to it.

There are lots of other activities I enjoy: hiking, biking, skiing, and tennis. But nothing can quite compare to going for a run—getting out there on the trail, heart pumping, sweat dripping, muscles flexing, adrenaline rushing, and energy flowing. It's like nothing else!

Ideas to Consider and Share

Why do you do what you do? How does it act as a release for you?

Share your stories on Instagram, Facebook, Twitter, and Strava.

Chapter Thirty-One

RUNNING AROUND

When you're busy, you don't have time to dwell on the past.

Running and training and working and parenting and husband-ing and traveling and maintaining friendships and writing and paying bills and taking care of the house and getting ready for another marathon are just parts of life.

I chuckle when people ask me if I was working full time during my marathon year. Of course, I still worked full time, slept part time, and did everything else I had to do as a human. Some months were way busier than others, and August was one of those months.

The Santa Rosa Marathon was on the schedule, and having already run that race twice previously, my confidence level was high. The course was familiar; it was only an hour drive from my house, a buddy of mine was going to run with me, and I'd had a solid month since my last race in July. Then the universe happened.

Since my first book, *Kids Deserve It!*, came out, I've started doing some speaking and traveling, which has been a rewarding experience. Having the opportunity to meet educators from around the country and work with school districts is an honor and a ton of fun. About five months before Santa Rosa, my agent booked some speaking in Minnesota for August, two days in a row at three different school districts. And the universe decided to plan them the day after my marathon. Yup, I was going to race in the morning, jam to the airport, fly to Minnesota, drive two hours, speak, drive another ninety minutes the next day, speak, do the same again, fly home to California, and be back to work the next day. And my next marathon was ten days after Santa Rosa.

I'd be running around for sure. Let's do this.

August in California can be hot, and it can be especially warm in Santa Rosa. At the race expo, picking up my bib and bottle of wine (At Mile 10, the course runs through a winery's tasting room.), the temperature gauge said it was 105 degrees. Race day was going to be hot, and I chugged water and stayed hydrated as well as I could. It was great hanging out with my buddy, who had originally signed up for the full but bumped his registration down to the half marathon because he didn't have the training to go 26.2 miles. There were also rumors at the expo that, because of the heat, the race organizers were going to start an hour early. I kept my fingers crossed for that option because I had such little time to race and catch my flight.

To tell you the truth, I was pretty worried about catching my flight, and there was only one backup flight, which landed after midnight. I also had dinner plans in Minnesota with a friend who was driving two hours to meet me. I had to make that flight.

The Santa Rosa Marathon is a terrific local race that's on the smaller side. The course runs through wineries and lots of farmland, and the full course goes through the DeLoach winery tasting room, where the winemakers are always passing out shots of Chardonnay. I've never taken one but have seen people partake, which I can't believe because we still have sixteen miles to go. Whatever gets you across the finish line. But now to the starting line.

From the beginning, it was difficult. Something happened at the start, and we were delayed fifteen minutes, which further clogged my race mojo.

I joined my usual 3:45 pace group and settled in on the course. The pacer was actually the same guy from last year, so we knew each other and enjoyed some casual conversation over the first few miles. Once I start a race, my focus is on the race, my body, nutrition, hydration, weather, which side of the road I run on, average pace per mile, and anything else that's on my mind. But my post-race travel was foremost on my mind. The thing with a marathon is you can't just run faster and finish when you want. So much can, and does, happen over all those miles. My body felt great, no aches or pains, and I'd recently hired a coach to help me finish out the year. But it was still a marathon, and you must always respect the marathon.

We passed through the tasting room at Mile 10, and our group was fully intact. As predicted, the winemakers were there passing out shots of Chardonnay. The temperature was in the low 90s—and thankfully, the course wound through country roads with an abundance of shade trees. The clock was on my mind, but I was able to gradually push away concerns about travel. If I missed my flight at 3:30 p.m., I'd catch the later one and deal with it in Minnesota.

If you can't control a situation, don't worry about the situation.

With six miles to go, we hopped back on a paved trail for the home stretch. I'd lost the 3:45 pace group a few miles back and was on my own. By this time, it was about ninety-five degrees. I crossed the line in 4:02 and kept racing—to the airport.

I grabbed my medal, filled up the water bottle, grabbed a banana, and ran to my car, which was parked a half mile away. There are always clean clothes in my marathon bag, but I didn't even bother. My shoes and socks were off, along with my shirt. I jumped in and started driving home in just my race shorts, without any shoes.

With the delay at the start, it was now almost noon, I had an hour drive ahead of me to my house, my flight took off at 3:30 p.m., and it was a forty-five-minute drive to the airport from my house.

Now maybe you're thinking, *Adam, why didn't you bring everything you needed to the race and drive straight to the airport?*

I thought about that. But I didn't want to deal with long-term parking and get on an airplane stinky, sweaty, and salty, and then meet my friend for dinner. I needed a shower, and that was happening at home.

My bag was already packed and ready to roll with everything I'd need for a three-day speaking trip in Minnesota. About fifteen minutes from home, I called my wife, asking her to blend me up a smoothie that I could take on the road. I remember walking in my front door at 1:05 p.m. I dropped my race bag and hopped in the shower. I was dressed in comfy flying clothes by 1:10. My smoothie was done, I started sucking that down, and ordered my Uber, which was seven minutes away. I did one last check of my bags, gave my family a kiss, and was in the car at 1:18.

Was I relieved? A little bit, but I still needed to catch my flight. My Uber driver came through in the clutch, and we made it to SFO at 2:30, which was still tight for my 3:30 flight, but I caught it without any trouble.

I woke up early the next morning for the two-hour drive north of Minneapolis for my first keynote of the trip. I had a great time with a really special school district that is doing amazing work for kids and repeated the schedule the next day with two keynotes at two different school districts about fifty miles apart. I again had to jam to the airport, so I could catch my flight home to California.

Was I tired? Of course, I was. Would I do it again? Say when, and I'll be there. What did I learn from this experience? A lot.

Our bodies are capable of so much more than what we normally put them through. The perceived limits that we impose are simply that—*perceived* limits. The connection between our brain and our body is so strong. Your body may tell you to stop, to quit, to give up, or to rest. But when you've trained your brain, it tells you something different. It tells you this: *you have more capacity, you have more steps, you have more energy, you have more in the tank that you didn't think was there, but you do.*

Push yourself and see what you're truly capable of. Because if you never put yourself in a situation that makes you nervous or uncomfortable or simply questions your ability to finish, you'll never know. As humans it's imperative we dig and scratch and claw and sometimes crawl our way forward. Because when you're finished, you'll look back and see what you've accomplished and maybe not even believe it yourself.

Running around is good for you. Try it sometime!

#RunLAP Reflections from Sarah Johnson
Principal, Wisconsin, @SarahSajohnson

When I started my runstreak on July 11, 2014, I never planned to run for three years straight. It was something I began during a challenging time in life, in an effort to find space for myself where there was none. Over the past three years, I have run every single day regardless of weather. Some days I was ill, but I ran. Sometimes I pounded out one to two miles with a 102-degree fever because running was the only time I felt well from those endorphins.

Throughout life's challenges—like losing a beloved brother to suicide, incredible levels of stress at work, lack of balance, and subsequent challenges at home—I ran through it. Gradually, and without even realizing it, I was beginning to lead with running. People around me asked for running updates, and many began their own goals, citing my streak as inspiration. "If you can do it, so can I!" they told me.

Within the past two years, I have placed in a local 5K, run a half-marathon with four principals, and completed two full marathons. With the help of my #EnduranceEducators PLN, I am fortified to continue.

The three-year ticker just elapsed, and I'm not sure what this year will bring. But I know that running has helped me be a better leader and a more reflective, healthy, balanced, and centered person. Running allows me to inspire, role model, and influence. Leading through running is something I didn't plan, but it is one of the most fulfilling ways that I impact my life and those in my circle.

Ideas to Consider and Share

When is a time you really pushed yourself? Was it out of your comfort zone physically, mentally, or both?

Share your stories on Instagram, Facebook, Twitter, and Strava.

#RUNLAP

PUSH YOURSELF AND SEE WHAT YOU'RE TRULY CADABLE OF.

Chapter Thirty-Two

WHAT YOU THINK YOU CAN'T

The only opinion that really matters is yours. Go do what you think you can't.

"**Y**ou should run a marathon!" I blurted.

"Oh no, not me," replied my colleague.

"Haven't you run a few half marathons?"

"I've done fifteen of them."

"How can someone who's run fifteen half marathons think they can't run and finish a full marathon?" I fumed. "You can totally run a full!"

"I don't think I could. It scares me."

What's stopping you? Do you think you aren't fast enough? Do you think people are going to laugh at you? Do you really think there aren't people out there who are slower than you? Even if you finish last, you finish!

Nobody is judging you. Nobody is talking about you.

Please try and do what you think you can't.

TRY SOMETHING NEW THAT PUSHES YOUR COMFORT ZONE.

Ideas to Consider and Share

What's something you've been thinking about for a while but haven't tried? What's holding you back? Who's putting those limits on you?

Share your stories on Instagram, Facebook, Twitter, and Strava.

#RUNLAP

Chapter Thirty-Three

NIGHT SWEATS

A marathon at night in the dark?
Sounds awesome!

Everyone I told about my September race gave me a sideways look. *Why would you want to run a marathon at night, on trails, in the dark, up and down lots of hills?*

The only two people who thought it was a brilliant idea were my coach and my friend James—who saw my racing schedule for the year in a post on the Brooks Running blog and texted me.

"Bro, I'd love to join you for that night marathon! Can I?"

"Are you kidding? I'd love to have someone run with me!"

And it was done. I had a partner in crime for my ninth marathon of the year and had a feeling that I would need the company.

The Night Sweats course has amazing views. It's across from San Francisco on the opposite side of the Golden Gate Bridge. The race starts at Fort Cronkhite, which is a World War II era outpost that's no longer used by the Army. Something else special about this race is the parking lot. Yes, the parking lot. We parked in the same lot where my buddy Frank I and parked for that North Face race where I met my wife. This was going to be a special night.

Leading up to race night, I felt really strong. I'd been taking about three days off after each marathon, but this one was happening so soon after Santa Rosa I didn't have that luxury. I took only one day off after that race and was in full marathon training mode, with lots of hill work.

You have more capacity inside of you, you have more to give, you have more energy than you think, you can do more than what you've done before. Trust me.

As you know by now, I have a pattern with marathons: 3:45 is usually my goal time but not for this one. My legs felt good but weren't fresh. My buddy trained hard but was nursing an Achilles' injury, which could slow us down. And there were those hills. My guess was we'd be somewhere between 4:45 and 5:00 for this race.

As usual, race day was pretty nuts. Another pattern. I was coaching my daughter's first grade soccer team that year, and we had a game the same day as Night Sweats. Of course, our game was the last one of the day at 3:00 p.m., so I put my coaching hat on, focused on soccer, got home by 4:30 p.m., and ate some breakfast food. This meal choice was something totally new for me at this time of day, but because of the night race, I was trying to keep a familiar schedule. I napped for an hour, got dressed, and was ready to roll.

September's weather in the Bay Area is usually nice and can also be hot. When James and I left my house, the temperature was in the mid-eighties, but when we pulled into the parking lot, things had cooled down quite a bit. I hadn't brought a jacket, or a vest, or even gloves. It was windy and about forty degrees at the start. The course hugs the San Francisco Bay, and the fog had rolled in. I wasn't really concerned about being cold because, once I get going, my body temperature ratchets up, and I'm fine. But something we hadn't thought about was the fog and what it would be like to run on a single-track at night with almost zero visibility.

This race was pretty low budget but well organized. There was also a 100-miler who had started the same morning who was using the same course. We were doing the loop once; he (or she) was doing it four times. At 8:00 we were off.

We ran straight up a hill and into the clouds—with about five feet of visibility on the trail. This was a small race, and about sixty people started, so it wasn't hectic on the trail. We just couldn't see anything.

And all I could do was smile. This is why I run. Why I run different races, at different times of day, with different variables I can't anticipate. Because it keeps things fresh and new.

The race was fun, and a slog, but mostly fun. James and I couldn't see a thing for most of the course, but it didn't really matter. We had each other, and that was enough. At a few points during the race, we heard waves crashing directly to our left—a reminder we were on single-track only a few feet from a hundred-foot cliff that dropped down to the ocean. We thought it was cool.

With about six miles to go, we ran up and over the crest that looked directly onto the Golden Gate bridge. It was well past midnight, the clouds had parted, and we were treated to a magnificent view of the iconic bridge. The sight lifted our spirits and helped us to finish those last miles.

With all the variables that were known and those that weren't, we were both stoked to finish no matter what our time was. Was I disappointed with 6:02? Not really. This race was about doing something different—about running every step with a good friend who was dealing with pain most of the way.

Try something new that pushes your comfort zone and internal systems, so they have no default to fall back on. That's what makes you stronger and better prepared for next time. That's the focus.

Ideas to Consider and Share

When was the last time you pushed yourself to try something new? To go outside of your comfort zone? How did it all work out?

Share your stories on Instagram, Facebook, Twitter, and Strava.

#RUNLAP

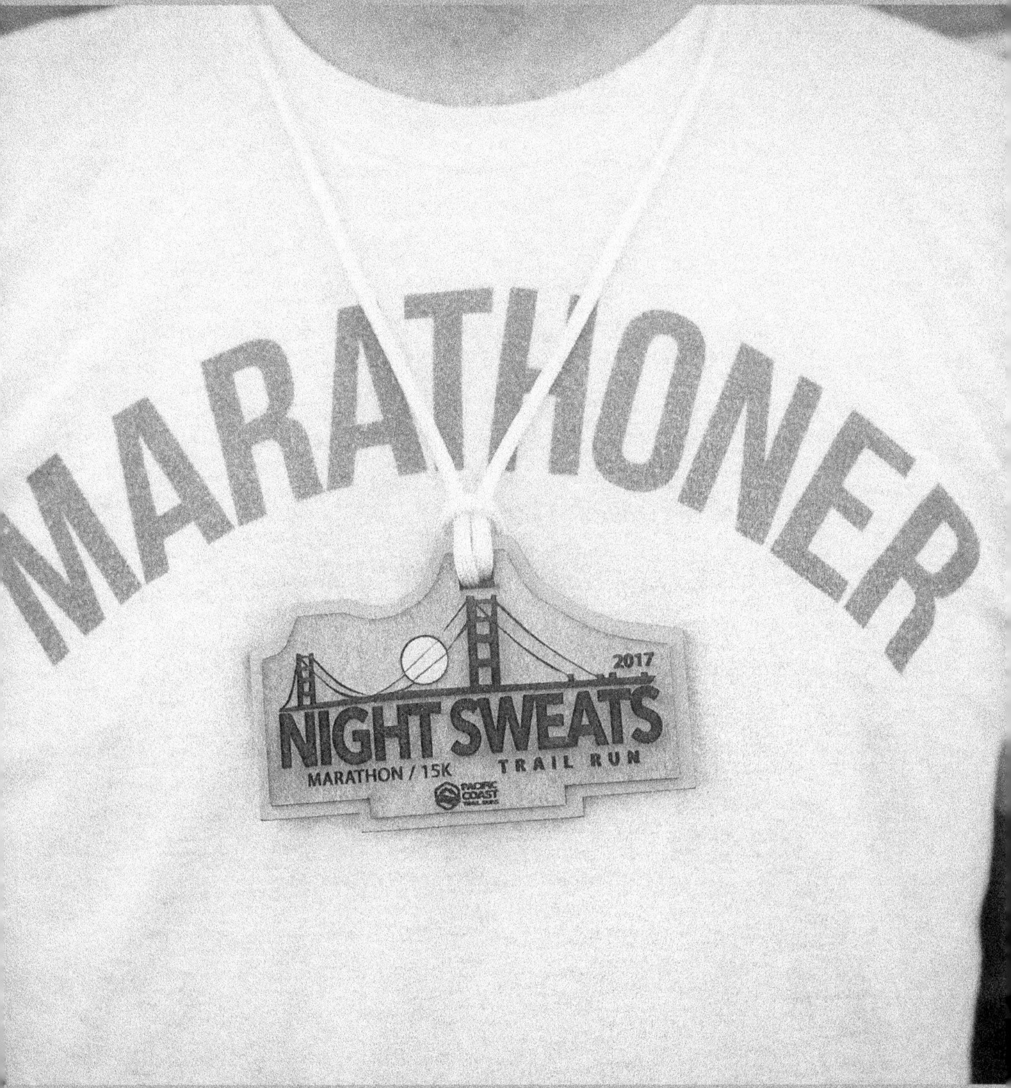
MARATHONER
2017
NIGHT SWEATS
TRAIL RUN
MARATHON / 15K

BEING COMFORTABLE WITH
DISCOMFORT IS IMPORTANT;
IT DOESN'T HAPPEN
OVERNIGHT, BUT IT NEEDS
TO HAPPEN AT SOME POINT.

Chapter Thirty-Four

It's Your Race

Forget what others are doing.
Focus on you.

It's easy to get wrapped in what's going on around you. You made a plan that fit your training and fitness level and feel good about where you are. You've been consuming certain foods and electrolyte drinks and have the nutrition you need. The gear you have will work for the conditions on race day. And then it happens.

You start second-guessing yourself. I've done it too many times.

It's the weather that usually shakes things up. Maybe you always run in the morning at home and are comfortable with shorts, a short sleeve shirt, your normal socks, a hat, and some gloves. Then race day happens. There's a slight chance of rain later in the morning, and the forecast throws your game plan into a tizzy. Should you wear a jacket? It's rainy and not too cold, but maybe you should wear some tights?

There have been times when I still haven't made up my mind the morning of a race. I've seen people wear waterproof rain jackets with the slightest amount of rain coming down. When you run a marathon, you sweat, a lot. You're going to get wet anyway. When you run 26.2

miles in a waterproof jacket that doesn't breathe, you're going to sweat even more; leave the jacket at home and trust in how you trained.

Food is the next variable that can throw people off kilter. If you've trained for the marathon, you've eaten a lot before the long runs—and during all those training runs as well—you're dialed in. You don't need to eat "extra" the night before or the morning of the race.

If you've trained with a certain type of gel, I highly discourage people from eating a completely different brand or flavor. All of this sampling should happen in training runs, so you can work out the kinks at home, not at Mile 20 of the race.

One of the worst mistakes I've seen people make is who they run with and how fast they go during a race. I ran a marathon years ago, and for some insane reason, I had the idea that I could run a 3:00 marathon. Up until that point, I hadn't run faster than 3:47. I was not in amazing shape, and I hadn't done any speed work. I did know who the pacer was, so maybe that's why I felt I could somehow keep up.

I hung with the group until Mile 16 and then completely fell apart. I got sick, had to walk for about half a mile, and never completely recovered. The final miles were no fun at all.

I've seen people change their strategy in the middle of race. We'll be cruising along with a happy pace group. Then people will run up next to us asking what group we're with. Someone will tell them, and then they'll freak out because they're "behind" and start sprinting. You should never be sprinting in a marathon unless you're in the Olympics and about to take over the person in front of you for a gold medal.

There is so much that changes throughout a race this long. Racers need to take a deep breath, calm down, and take back time in small increments. Trust in your training and run your own race at the pace you should be running—not what others around you are running.

At the end of the day, I always remind myself:

I'm doing this for me.

I'm not running for friends.

It's not my job.

I'm not trying to impress anyone.

I'm not running for the medal.

I'm doing this for me—to quench my own desires and goals and to learn from the internal battle that happens during 26.2 miles down the road. Everyone runs for different reasons. My recommendation is to develop discipline in your training, so that on race day, you have an enjoyable experience and don't second-guess yourself. It's your race: go enjoy!

#RunLAP Reflections from Pam Hernandez
Principal, New Jersey, @pamhernandez_4

A Chromebook is one hundred times more powerful than a pencil. As the principal of the John F. Kennedy Elementary school in Jamesburg, New Jersey, I knew our superstar students needed more opportunities to become connected, but it always came back to a lack of finances. *But what can one principal do to raise enough money for much-needed technology?*

Along with a committee of PTA members, a board of education member, and teachers, I brainstormed ways to raise enough money to get some Chromebooks for our students. How about a pancake breakfast or a pasta dinner? Maybe a Tricky Tray? For the kind of money needed to really make a difference, those weren't options.

I frequently went home feeling frustrated because of the lack of funding for technology. I heard about other amazing individuals who tapped into fundraising sites with worthwhile personal causes and thought, *That's it! I can run a marathon to raise a substantial amount of dinero!* But could I really run 26.2 miles when I've never run more than five miles in one stretch in the fifty-fourth year of my life? My husband spent much of his life as a passionate runner, so he was my go-to guy. He assured me that if I trained properly, I could do it. Before I could think too long about the implications, I secured permission from my superintendent, signed up for the New Jersey Marathon (which was six months away), and created the "Run All Day for JFK" fundraising page and a "Run All Day for JFK" Facebook page.

Instantly, my husband jumped in and took me on as his project. Over the years, I have enlisted his help with the project du jour that ensured positive outcomes for my superstar students. From filling water balloons on Field Day, to building a book room for my teachers, to training me for a marathon, I have always counted on him! Through frosty mornings, weekend afternoons, star-lit evenings, and everything in between, I ran under his tutelage that winter.

Awesome teachers, friends, and families shared the fundraiser on their Facebook pages and Twitter accounts, and the pledges rolled in. We held assemblies, pumping up the students and letting them know about the progress of our fundraising efforts. We sold Run All Day for JFK t-shirts, and the students wore them at our JFK Fun Run before the marathon. The local police blocked off the streets, parent volunteers were stationed along the route, and our superstar students had fun running in our school neighborhood!

A few days later, on a windy spring morning, I set out to accomplish this venture for my superstar students. My daughter posted updates on social media so that the JFK families could see my progress. At Mile 12, my husband jumped in and ran with me for five miles, and my daughter took over at Mile 17 to partner with me for the last nine miles of the run. I ran all day for JFK, and we raised enough money to purchase thirty extra Chromebooks and a charging station for my JFK superstars! Beyond the obvious material gain, my superstar students had the opportunity to see firsthand that, if you set a goal and work towards it in a collaborative manner, you can accomplish anything.

Ideas to Consider and Share

What does it mean to you to run, to hike, to be outside, to follow your passion?

Share your stories on Instagram, Facebook, Twitter, and Strava.

#RUNLAP

TRY BIG THINGS TO SEE
WHAT HAPPENS. THAT'S THE
ONLY WAY YOU'RE GOING
TO FIND OUT WHAT YOU
HAVE INSIDE.

Chapter Thirty-Five

Smoke and Elevation

If you always run the same course,
you'll always get the same results.

*O*h boy, was I ready for October to come around. My legs were so stiff and sore from the night marathon that it hurt to walk for an entire week. The ups and downs trashed my legs, so I took off four entire days from doing anything. I felt fresh and ready for the Lake Tahoe Marathon.

October in Lake Tahoe is amazing. I've been going to the mountains my entire life, and we're very lucky to have a family cabin, so we spend many weekends at the lake, and the course was very familiar. One variable I couldn't predict: the wildfires that were raging in northern California.

Not too far from my home in the Bay Area, wildfires had devastated many communities in Sonoma County and other surrounding areas. The fires were raging about seventy miles from my home, but there was an intense wind that amplified the speed of the fires and how they spread. These winds also pushed much of that smoke into the Bay Area. The smoke was actually so bad that many school districts (including my own) canceled school for a couple of days because air-quality levels were in the extreme range.

With all this going on, I still had to train. My wife and I don't own a treadmill, but she does work in emergency medicine and picked up a couple of high quality masks (N95) for us to wear. You got it; I wore a facemask during my training runs for about ten days. Early in the morning seemed to be the best time of day. I'm sure the smoke was there, but when it's cool and crisp at 4:00 a.m., you couldn't see it, taste it, or smell it. But it was hard to breathe in that mask.

The first half mile wasn't bad, but once you start breathing heavy and your body starts to sweat, that mask gets nasty. You have to take small breaths and pull it off every half mile or so to take a small suck of air then quickly put it back on. Was I being stupid running outside with air-quality levels in the extreme zone? Truthfully, I don't know. I looked into buying a treadmill for the week, but it didn't make sense, so I made it work with the mask.

Training that week wasn't the only consideration. What was I going to do about the marathon that weekend? Lake Tahoe is a couple hundred miles from where the main fires were, but some other fires had now started in a different location, and we were at the mercy of the strong winds. If the smoke was too intense in Tahoe, I was going to skip the race. I was cool with doing some training runs wearing a mask in the smoke but not a full marathon.

I had to run one this month to keep my marathon streak alive. For contingency planning, I did a quick search for other races happening in the next couple weeks, and the options were not good. I emailed a few neighbors and asked if they had treadmills, in case I needed to run 26.2 miles inside, but none were available.

Wait and see. Make a game-time decision. Hope for the best.

Two days before the race, I searched every "live cam" I could find online in the Lake Tahoe area to see what the air looked like. I checked air-quality levels and race updates from the director. If canceled, I would pay for a one-day pass to a local gym and run my October marathon on a treadmill.

Thankfully I didn't have to. The race was on!

The air was clear but cold. So cold in the morning at lake level that our start got bumped an hour later. *I'll take it,* I thought.

The Lake Tahoe marathon is a point-to-point course and runs along the lake—around Emerald Bay, which is a simply magical place and one of the most beautiful spots on the planet and where we would pick up the half marathon runners for the final 13.1 miles. We then run through historic Camp Richardson, around the Tahoe Keys, and then hop on the multi-use trail for the final miles around the lake, finishing on the beach near the California and Nevada state line.

When I hopped in my car to drive over and catch the bus to the start, it was eighteen degrees. We were two hours away from the start, but the sun probably wasn't going to be up in time for that, and we'd have to grin and bear with tight muscles.

Most marathons that bus you to the start allow you to stay on as long as you want before start time, but not this one. They dropped us off and went back to pick up the half marathoners to get them where they needed to be. We were still ninety minutes away from starting, and there wasn't much we could do to stay warm, except think warm thoughts.

I walked back and forth at the start in a futile attempt to keep some blood flowing through my body.

The race director grabbed a shotgun, loaded a blank shell, fired his weapon, and we were off! There was also a guy playing bagpipes as we started down the road, which was pretty cool. By the time we finally started, I couldn't feel my toes and it hurt to run. The first three miles felt like I was running on bricks with hundreds of needles sticking my feet. Time to revert to my training, put a frozen smile on my face, enjoy the beautiful surroundings, and be thankful I can run a marathon.

Focus on what you can control and not on what you can't.

The other factor on my mind was how many calories I'd burned at the start trying to stay warm. I've read about this a lot over the years, and all the shivering and mental focus on trying to stay warm can actually burn lots of calories. This cold "hang out" before the start was new, and I was afraid there weren't enough calories in my body to get me through.

Don't worry about that, Adam. Get warmed up and figure it out on the course.

I'd previously run almost the entire course, knew all the hills, and did pretty well with elevation. My time goal was not the usual 3:45. I figured between 4:05 and 4:15 because the hills and elevation would slow me down. We made our way through the course, and the miles were ticking off pretty nicely. That calorie deficit from the start was still on my mind, and I grabbed some extra food at an aid station and made a mental note on how much I'd eaten and body logistics for later in the race.

We made our way up the steepest and longest hill of the race, then a slight downhill around Emerald Bay, and a small climb to a beautiful crest where the half marathoners were about to start. Just as I was getting to the half marathon start, I heard the shotgun blast again. They were off, and I was enveloped by a throng of runners starting on the course.

I'd felt strong up until this point, but just as we were making the first descent into Camp Richardson, I started to get that feeling—that feeling when your brain has one agenda but your legs have another. There weren't any official pacers in this race, and since I was running solo, I slowed down and took an assessment.

My feet were no longer frozen. Check.

My heart rate felt normal, and I was not redlining at all. Check.

I'd been eating and added additional calories for what I lost during the cold start. Check.

About eleven miles to go at this point. Check.

I just needed to keep going and get this race done. But in the back of my mind, I knew what it was: the two weeks of running in the smoke with a mask. I'm sure it inhibited my training. It was also the elevation where we were running, which is over 6,000 feet. I've run in Tahoe hundreds of times throughout my life but never a marathon there.

It all caught up with me, and there was only one thing to do. Keep moving, one foot in front of the other. I was getting exactly what I asked for: pain.

The last few miles of that race were definitely a trudge fest, but I got it done in 4:19, not too far from my goal. My body was tired, I was hungry, I missed my family, and I still had a four-hour drive home. I grabbed my medal and a fresh bottle of water, walked the mile to my car, and started driving home.

Sometimes I grab something to eat for the road, but this time I just wanted to get home. That's not unusual; I've never stayed to hang out after the race. The marathon is a job, and when I'm finished with the job, I go home. I finish and then look ahead to what's next.

And I had some mental work to do. My November race would be the biggest so far, and it was only three weeks away. New York was going to be huge in so many ways, and I was looking for some much-needed redemption.

Ideas to Consider and Share

What are some struggles you've faced throughout your life? How did you handle them? What did you learn?

Share your stories on Instagram, Facebook, Twitter, and Strava.

#RUNLAP

Chapter Thirty-Six

If I Can and They Can, Then You Can

**All you need to do is look around.
Trust me; you got this.**

Yes, I've been an athlete most of my life, but I wasn't always a "runner" as I would define myself today. I played baseball; we ran the bases. In basketball, we'd run up and down the court. But running a marathon is completely different.

If you think you can't, you're completely wrong.

If I can do it, and the other runners on the course can do it, then you can do it too.

Maybe you have an image of what a runner should look like. It's wrong. You need to recalibrate. Anyone who has the desire and will to train, take care of their body, prepare by doing the right things, and adopt the mindset that they're going to finish, can and will. That's what a runner looks like.

For example, this happens all the time: at Mile 24, I get passed by a runner who's at least seventy years old. As I write this, I'm thirty-eight, and I often get beat by someone in their sixties or seventies. It always makes me smile and is such a great reminder. Never assume, never judge, never doubt, never think they can't, never have preconceived notions of what a runner looks like. And never think that you're past your prime and only have a few years left. That's garbage.

People try to tell me how bad running is for you. Oh really? Tell it to that grandmother who passed me at Mile 24. Tell that to all the ultra runners who run a hundred miles every week in their training.

They do exactly what I do: start and finish. When you have the determination to start and finish, you've won. That's it.

Because if I can, and they can, you can do it too.

#RunLAP Reflections from Andrea Flores
Teacher, California, @mrsandreaflores

My love for running started as a young child, while watching my parents. They ran almost daily, and in the odd chance they didn't run together, they would discuss their daily runs at dinner, while recapping their day. My parents not only taught me how to have a love for each other, but they taught me to love running.

My first running partner was my mother. We started running together around the track when I was in fifth grade. I wasn't a serious runner like she was. I ran, stopped, walked, sprinted to catch up with her again, then continued the pattern. My mother, who always made it look so easy, continued at the same pace and smiled at me when I caught up to her side.

One day in college, I told her that I wanted to run a marathon, and being the best running partner a girl could ask for, she said, "Let's do it!" We joined a marathon training club in San Diego. Every weekend we ran our long runs with the group. As I ran beside her,

I couldn't help but think that she must be really proud that I wasn't that middle school girl anymore at our neighborhood track.

Three months later, we ran our first marathon, Rock 'n' Roll San Diego, and crossed the finish line hand-in-hand. This race will forever be my favorite, not necessarily for the course, but for the company.

Ideas to Consider and Share

Has there been a time when you've been surprised by what others around you can do? Or have done? Did it motivate you in anyway?

Share your stories on Instagram, Facebook, Twitter, and Strava.

#RUNLAP

IT'S TIME FOR THE TRAINING WHEELS TO COME OFF. THEY'RE A CRUTCH AND SLOWING YOU DOWN; TAKE THEM OFF AND GO GET AFTER IT.

Chapter Thirty-Seven

THE WORK

It's what you do when everyone else is asleep that matters.

It's more difficult than you think it's going to be. But it's way more fun than what you expect.

You're gonna hurt. You're gonna throw up. Your brain is going to be tired. You're not gonna want to get up all the time to train. You may even question yourself along the journey.

Regardless, if you want to cross that finish line, you have to put in the work. If you try to fake it, the course will slap you in the face when it's game time.

Maybe you have enough discipline on your own. You can get through tough situations without help from others. I've done that myself—on rare occasions. But I've always found that having accountability from family and friends is a tremendous bonus.

Accountability is the difference between just having goals and taking action toward them. When you make things public, tell your friends, or post on social media, it's real. And people will hold you accountable. They'll also encourage you when they know what you're trying to accomplish.

The Los Angeles Marathon was a tough one for me, as you read earlier in the book. It was pretty early in my marathon year, but people knew what I was doing. I blogged about it. Tweeted it. Posted photos on Instagram. And even talked about it on podcasts where I was a guest. Lots of people knew what I was after.

In the middle of that race, I posted photos of my struggle. And the messages started to come in.

"You got this, Adam. Keep going!"

"Don't give up; you're more than halfway done."

"One foot in front of the other is all it takes!"

Supporters on social media, some I knew and many I didn't, held me accountable. I couldn't drop out of the race. And there was no way my accountability partners would let that happen.

Find your crew, connect with them, make your goals and ambitions public, and they'll be there for you. We can't do this alone. And sometimes that means hiring a coach.

All year my training had been going really well. I was consistent, disciplined, eating vegan, throwing in long runs on the weekend. And then I started to think about December. In July of 2017, I decided it was time to hire a coach. I'd run a slew of marathons that year, but I had some big days coming up in December, and I needed help. Hiring a coach was a pivotal moment for my marathon year, and it's when the work got real.

The first week with my coach resulted in a ten percent increase in what my usual training had been. But on week two, I went from running three to five miles, four days per week, to running six to eight miles with *fartlek* runs and hill repeats thrown in on Monday through Friday. And my weekend training changed drastically too. I'd been throwing down a ten or thirteen miler most weekends, and it went up from there. The mileage wasn't a big deal; it was the repeat days, one after another after another. She called it "seasoning my legs," which is a phrase I still use today. I only had two days off per month, and I loved it!

It wasn't that I wouldn't have done the mileage on my own; it was the structure that I was after. I was staring down a double marathon in December, where I planned to run the race backward in the middle of the night at 1:00 a.m. then turn around to run the real race with everyone else an hour later. I also entered a twenty-four-hour race on New Year's Eve from 9 a.m. to 9 p.m. to see how far I could go in that time. I had to ramp up my workload. December was going to be real.

If you want results, if you want to achieve big things, if you want to see those goals that you made come to fruition, putting in the work is the only answer.

Here was a typical week.

Monday: 8-mile run.

I'd wake up at 4:00 a.m., run, be home by 5:45 a.m. to make school lunches for my kids, get breakfast ready for them, shower, get ready for work, take my daughter to school, work all day, come home to hang with the family, sometimes moderate a Twitter chat or record a podcast, get my kids ready for bed, check emails and other related computer stuff, read for thirty minutes, and then head to bed around 9:00 or 9:30 p.m.

Tuesday: 6- to 8-mile *fartlek* run.

Repeat the non-training stuff listed above.

Wednesday: 8- to 10-mile run with four to six 20-second sprints at the end.

Repeat the life agenda!

Thursday:	6-mile run, slow and steady not worrying about pace. Yes, repeat above.
Friday:	8-mile run at race pace. Repeat, repeat, repeat.
Saturday:	14- to 18-miler, sometimes a 30 or 35 when we got closer to December.

I still wake up at 4:00 a.m. to run before the family wakes up. I'm a firm believer in "dark miles" and training when they're asleep, so I don't miss out on family time.

Soccer games, gymnastics, skiing in Lake Tahoe, birthday parties, pool time during the summer, sometimes traveling for speaking or conferences.

Sunday:	Repeat, repeat, repeat.

The work is fun. It really is. It's just not glamorous. You're going to be cold, lonely, tired, frustrated, and stuck in the rain. Even with all the reflective gear on the market, cars are going to buzz you, throw stuff at you, and even yell at you. There will be days when that alarm goes off, and you'll need to rip yourself out of bed. The training struggle is very real.

And that is exactly why setting goals, making them public, and having a team around you is so very important. Without all of those factors, failure is just around the corner.

Quite a few times, I "changed" up my training and would go to bed at 9:00 p.m., wake up at midnight, and go run in the middle of the night. Running ten miles at midnight is an awesome experience. It trains you to not have a routine. It trains you to run with different food in your stomach and without enough sleep. Fatigue training is powerful training. It shows your body that you can handle something different because there will be a time in a race when you'll need to make that call to your body and ask for something it's not accustomed to giving.

Be obsessive about the work. Always bring your goals back to the conversation. And don't forget to smile. A smile always helps—even in the dark!

Ideas to Consider and Share

What do you love about the work? Do you have some room to improve? What's your biggest challenge with getting it all done?

Share your stories on Instagram, Facebook, Twitter, and Strava.

#RUNLAP

KEEP IT SIMPLE. THE
MORE COMPLICATED
THINGS ARE, THE MORE
THAT CAN GO WRONG.
LIGHT AND TIGHT IS
HOW I ROLL.

Chapter Thirty-Eight

It's Your Turn Now

**Many before you have done it.
Now it's your turn.**

t's lonely being on the sidelines, watching other people in the game, seeing them build relationships with their team, getting stronger in their body and mind. Stop waiting around; it's your turn now.

Why do people wait and not get involved? Is it fear? Lack of self-discipline? Not enough confidence in their own abilities? Maybe it's none, or all, of those things. But whatever it is, it stifles forward progress.

Stop thinking you're not fast enough or worthy of being in the game because you are. It's your turn now.

My parents were amazing. They signed me up for events, encouraged me and pushed me further and higher than what I thought was possible. And I'm confident you can do it too. It's your turn now.

Don't be afraid to join in. Everyone in the group is just like you. Sure, they may have started a little earlier, but it's your turn now.

You may think they're staring at you and judging you, but I really doubt it. And if they are, who cares? Go out there. It's your turn now.

Ideas to Consider and Share

What exactly are you waiting for? Have you ever waited to do something, and it was too late? What can you change, so next time there's an opportunity you're ready and willing to go?

Share your stories on Instagram, Facebook, Twitter, and Strava.

#RUNLAP

Chapter Thirty-Nine

THE BIG APPLE

I don't sit and celebrate; I look ahead
to the work that's coming next.

A marathon is a marathon, but November was going to be special. Ever since I met my wife, she talked about this legendary race. It was her favorite marathon ever—the crowds, the bridges, and the city. She loved everything about it.

I'd put my name in for the lottery, and just before the Los Angeles Marathon, the email came in. I'd be running the New York City marathon in November, and I couldn't wait.

The original plan was to have the entire family come east for the race. We'd go a few days early, hang out in the city, and then I'd run. But then Grandma came through in the clutch, so Stacy and I could have a solo trip. We'd miss them, but it would be fun to have an adult weekend away, and the kids were stoked to camp out with the grandparents.

Prior to New York, the largest marathon I ran was in Los Angeles with over 20,000 runners, which felt like a huge race. New York has over 60,000 runners; it's the largest marathon in the world and attracts some world-class runners This would be a race to remember.

New York City is amazing—all the sights, people, restaurants, history. Throw in all the festivities for the marathon, and it's completely off the hook. I went to New York University for a semester when I was exploring graduate schools back in 2000. Being with my wife would make it even more fun. She wanted to explore, and I'm always ready for new adventures. My wife ran the marathon in 2008, but it was a quick trip with friends.

As you know, I'm not the kind of runner who stays off my feet for days before a race. I don't take it easy or try to "save my legs" for race day. If we're in New York for three days without the kids, we're going to see the city. And see the city we did. We walked and walked and walked. We hopped a ferry to the Statue of Liberty and walked some more. We spent hours at Ellis Island, read the history of our ancestors, and walked around. We walked to the 9/11 Memorial. We trekked across town to find a Whole Foods, so I could get pre-race snacks and a smoothie. (It had been a few days since my last spinach smoothie, and I was salivating for one.) We visited the Empire State Building (Yes, we took the elevator and not the stairs.) and took some awesome selfies on the observation deck. We even walked a couple of more miles to meet with people at Donors Choose to talk about upcoming opportunities and partnerships.

Our last pre-marathon trek was in search of a burrito. Some people eat pasta the night before a run; I eat a burrito. We walked around Manhattan so much that I ate two burritos. My legs felt solid, and I was ready to run!

The logistics of getting everyone to Staten Island for this race are insane. I was assigned the Midtown Manhattan bus, based on the location of our hotel. Race morning is always busy, but it's difficult to describe how intense that morning was. There was a breakfast set up for runners in our hotel, but the line was absolutely bonkers. As you know, I always leave lots of time before I need to be at the starting line, but I spent thirty minutes in this line and only moved a few feet. I weighed my options. I could stay in line for my ritual of oatmeal on race morning and still get to Staten Island in "enough" time for the race, or I could eat what I had in my bag and get to the start. I decided to leave.

Be flexible in your training, what you eat, when you eat, how you eat, and on race day—when things don't go exactly as planned—you'll be okay.

There was airport-level security at the starting villages, and the rows of buses leading up to Staten Island went on forever. When I say "villages," I mean just that. There were several different villages for all the runners, assigned based on bib number and starting position. They had free beanies for everyone, coffee from Dunkin' Donuts, hot chocolate, bagels, and huge loudspeakers greeting runners in at least six languages. It was a sight to be seen and very much an international affair.

The organizers stage runners early, due to the scale and logistics that go into putting on an event of this size. After hanging out for a couple of hours, we got the call to enter our starting corral. Based on my projected finish time of 3:45, I was in the first starting group and fourth corral. For some perspective, the final runners wouldn't even be starting their race until I was one hour and thirty minutes into mine. There would be a long line of runners weaving around New York for the entire day, and I couldn't even fathom the level of energy we were about to feel on the course.

Starting on the Verrazano Narrows Bridge (also known as the Staten Island Bridge), we broke up into two groups: top level of the bridge and bottom. My group was on the bottom, and we could see the elite females take off above us, about fifteen minutes ahead of everyone else. The buzz in the air was really something, not to mention the dozen helicopters buzzing overhead. My wife would be on the course around Mile 17 to cheer me on. It was go time, and I was ready.

Ever since the Los Angeles Marathon in March, I've carried my phone with me during races. It was an experiment in documenting each race on social media—from the start, during the race, and all the way across the finish line. I wasn't quite sure how posting photos and updates on Instagram and Twitter would work out as I ran, but it's been a rewarding experience with friends throughout the country tracking my progress throughout the year and during each race. New York wouldn't be any different, but I'd also be texting updates to my wife, so I could catch a glimpse of her on the course—if I could find her in the throng of people.

When you run the New York Marathon, you're never alone, ever. I've run plenty of marathons where there are no spectators for miles and miles and miles. In New York, you're always surrounded by other runners, and except for the five bridges, there are people lined up and down both sides of the street for the entire race from start to finish. It's like nothing I'd ever seen before; the energy of fellow runners and spectators takes you to a place of running euphoria I've never experienced. It's magical.

The miles were ticking off like any normal training run on the streets of my hometown—and nutrition, along with hydration, were totally on point.

My wife always says that no matter where we go, I see someone I know. (I once bumped into a friend in Barcelona, Spain!) And that's exactly what happened. Around Mile 10, I noticed a jersey for a running shoe store back home, where I worked at for many years, and I knew both runners—a husband and wife team. We ran together for quite a few miles. He was coming off an Ironman just a few weeks before, so I pushed on a little faster, and we continued on running our own races.

Soon after, I spotted someone else I knew. Actually, I spotted his jaw bone and running stride. I didn't really "know" him, but I could tell by those two features it was Dean Karnazes. I'd run with Dean the year before during a book signing at my local library, and to say he's been an influential figure in my own running would be an understatement. His books, his exploits, the running ambassador he is for the community is legendary, and he's a genuine guy. And I wanted a selfie.

I came up next to him and scouted the scene. He seemed to be by himself. He was looking around and not talking with anyone, so I struck up a conversation.

"Hey Dean, looking good!"

"Thanks, man. You too!"

Then he gave me a fist bump. *What?!*

"We're from the same hood, Dean. I live in the Bay Area also!"

"Nice, how you feeling?"

"Really strong. Hey . . . can I get a selfie?"

"For sure, if you can take it while we run."

And that's exactly what I did. What an amazing moment. We ran together for a couple of miles, chatted about different races in the Bay Area, and found out we'd be together again next month for the twenty-four-hour race on New Year's Eve. But now it was time to get back on track and focus on *this* marathon.

My wife texted me her location, and she was just a few miles ahead. The goal was to stop, get a kiss, and take a photo before continuing. You already know a little bit about Stacy and that she hates when I stop during a race. She's run-run-run during a marathon and all business. I take a slightly different approach. I knew where she was but wasn't sure if I'd be able to find her.

Looking, running, texting, searching, and there she was. Ringing a cowbell and smiling from ear to ear in the front row behind the barricade. I couldn't wait to see her.

"How you are feeling?"

"Really strong; this race is amazing!"

"Go, Honey, go!"

I grabbed a kiss, took a photo together, and looked forward to seeing her at the finish.

It was Mile 17, and the race was getting real. I checked Instagram and saw the women's finisher was already done, and it was none other than Shalane Flanagan—the first female American to win this race in over forty years. That put a smile on my face and added some fuel to my gas tank. I took stock of my body and felt confident. I'd been eating and drinking regularly, nothing hurt, and my calorie levels felt strong, so I turned the screws and starting running a little faster. There was only one *teeny, tiny, little climb* left as we made our way into Central Park, but I wasn't worried about it. I knew the downhill through the park, and the energy at the finish would help propel me through if I started feeling shaky.

There was little thought in the back of my brain about December. In just three weeks, I'd be running my December marathon, and it wouldn't be any ordinary race. I was running that course twice (52.4 miles) and, for a moment, thought about backing off my pace to conserve for December. Then I reminded myself of something very important. You only live once.

I was running this race right now. I still had three weeks to recover and prepare for the double marathon, and I kept going. Look ahead to the future and plan, but experience the now to your absolute fullest potential.

I did the math in my head as we approached the final miles and realized there was a chance I could break my personal marathon record of 3:36 from the previous year. My food was gone, and I was really sweating and starting to have concern about taking on enough liquids. I didn't want to bonk with just a couple of miles left.

One of the last aid stations was passing out some type of food, but I stuck to my training protocol and didn't eat anything that I hadn't trained with. Even this late in the race, eating something new to my body could throw off my internal systems, and I'd come so far, so fast, and didn't want to risk it.

In the end, I didn't push the pace those final couple of miles. I was tired but felt strong and wanted to finish classy without any issues in the home stretch. The last mile was a tunnel of sounds, energy, people, sweat, passion, and so many dreams coming true for so many people. Crossing that finish line in 3:38 felt more special than any of my previous races. I grabbed my medal, took an official race photo, and had an unusual feeling.

I felt like I could keep on running—and wanted to run some more. I tucked those feelings into my back pocket because I'd need them very soon.

My wife and I linked up at the reunion area and didn't really have too much time to chill. The feeling inside was amazing, and my wife was happy because I'd joined the New York club she'd been talking about for so many years. She may have also noted that her New York time was faster than mine. I really did marry the right woman. She's amazing and super-fast!

These feelings from New York were fabulous, but I couldn't dwell on them. I had work to do. We landed back in California at 11:00 p.m. I went to work the very next day and did a five-mile shakeout run that night.

I'd be running in the biggest game of my life in three short weeks.

Ideas to Consider and Share

Share a special moment you've had in your life. A big race? A huge accomplishment? How did it make you feel?

> Share your stories on Instagram, Facebook, Twitter, and Strava.
>
> **#RUNLAP**

IF YOU DON'T WANT TO
SEE WHAT YOU'RE MADE
OF, FINE, BUT I AM,
AND THEY ARE, SO YOU
MIGHT AS WELL.

Chapter Forty

USE YOUR BANDWIDTH

**You have so much more in your tank.
Dig deep down and achieve
your full potential.**

It's rampant in our society—an issue that people gloss over or don't even realize they have.

I'm talking about your bandwidth: the amount of energy and potential that you have inside your body, which often is not utilized.

"I've run a few 5K races, but I could never run a half marathon."

How do you know? When you make a statement like that, you take yourself out of the game. The more interactions I have with people on the subject, the more I'm convinced it's all based on fear. Fear that they won't finish. Fear of starting something new.

As you can tell, my family is quite active. We hike, ride bikes, snow ski, swim—you name it, and we do it. We'll even go to the high school track sometimes to run laps as a family. The school district where we live puts on a local race every year to raise money. There's a kids' run, a two-mile run, a 5K, and a 10K. A few years ago, when our kids were really little, we used to run the 5K and push them in the jogging stroller. As they got older, we'd run/walk the kids' run, finally making our way up to the two-mile. At ages three and five, our kids ran the entire two miles! My wife and I were super proud of them, and we let them know it.

Last year we told them it was time for the 5K. They wanted to run the two-mile. They argued. They complained. They lobbied us for the two-mile.

"We can't run a 5K, Dad!"

"You ran two miles last year, and a 5K is only one more mile," I replied.

The weird thing about this entire situation is that both our kids are tough. Yes, they complain at times, but they always get after it. We had to break through their fear and excuses.

"We're running the 5K as a family, and that includes both of you. Mom and I know you can run it because we've been on hikes that are twice as long as a 5K. You ran the two-mile last year and were barely breathing hard when we finished. We're running the 5K."

That's exactly what we did, and they were amazing. My son had his game face on during the entire race and didn't say a word except to ask for some water a couple of times. My daughter wouldn't stop talking. She was looking around. Looking for her friends. Telling us how much fun she was having and asking what we were eating for breakfast after the race. We were proud parents and definitely glowing after this one. They crossed the finish line after sprinting the final hundred yards.

What fascinates me, and also concerns me, are all those people who don't have that person in their life to help them find their full potential. I find it truly sad that people have what it takes to make the jump up, and many never do. They never find their full potential and tap into all the reserves that are just sitting there waiting to be utilized.

You have more bandwidth. Tap into it and see what you can do.

Ideas to Consider and Share

Are you operating at full capacity? If not, what's stopping you? Share about a time when you let it all hang out and gave it everything you had!

Share your stories on Instagram, Facebook, Twitter, and Strava.

#*RUNLAP*

THERE'S MORE; THERE'S ALWAYS MORE. SOMETIMES IT'S HIDDEN, AND YOU NEED TO GO FIND IT. SOMETIMES IT'S RIGHT IN FRONT OF YOU, AND YOU DON'T EVEN REALIZE IT. SOMETIMES THE JOURNEY IS NOT WHAT YOU'RE GOING TO EXPECT. BUT NO MATTER WHAT, THERE'S ALWAYS MORE.

Chapter Forty-One

MY CREW

I keep my circle pretty tight, so we don't
experience any leaks along the way.

Who's in your crew? Who keeps you running? Who helps fill your tank? Who's there during the tough times? Who can you count on when you need them most? Who knows exactly what you're going through, even if they're thousands of miles away?

Your crew is more important than you think, and maybe it's time to think about them in a different way.

My family is number one. My wife and two children offer unwavering support in whatever idea I come up with and pursue. They tell me I can. And that they love me. That they're proud of me. They believe. They sacrifice for all those early-morning and late-night runs and even those training runs when we're on vacation. I would probably never cross a finish line if it wasn't for my family. They are my main crew.

My friends come in many different forms. Some I work with on a daily basis. Some don't even run, but they support, encourage, and listen to my stories with a smile. They're always available if needed, and I know they truly care. They get encouraged by my exploits, and some turn over a new leaf to find a healthier and better self. For that I'm eternally grateful and happy.

The virtual friends in my circle are some of the most vital and influential. Most I've never met in person. We haven't even talked on the phone, but we're in constant communication. Updates on our training and races through social media apps bring us closer together now than at any other time in history. Twitter, Instagram, and Facebook are great, but Voxer is really my go-to app for staying connected with my virtual crew. (Think group text but in a cleaner and easier to use format.)

The *Run Like a Pirate* group I started on Voxer has grown to hundreds of members from all over the country, and we keep each other motivated and energized all year long. Find some friends and start a group. No matter what activity you choose, *virtual* friends are *really* important!

Think about your crew. Do they support you, or do they suck the life out of you? Life is too short and there are too many races to run. Find the crew that adds to your fuel tank. Because when that happens, you're better, you're healthier, you're stronger, you're more confident, and you have much more to give back.

Ideas to Consider and Share

Who's in your crew and why? What does your crew do for you? How do you help support your crew?

> Share your stories on Instagram, Facebook, Twitter, and Strava.
> **#RUNLAP**

Chapter Forty-Two

It's All Upstairs

I told myself I could, so I did.

As a father with two kids, we wrestle a lot at home; I've had my share of tickle sessions. Recently, my daughter stopped in the middle of one and asked a question.

"How come you're not ticklish, Dad?"

I knew that question was going to come up eventually. I paused and then explained. "Well, Greta, many years ago, I turned off my tickle."

"What? How do you do that?" she asked.

"No way," our son chimed in.

My wife was in the room and started to smile. She knew I wasn't ticklish and was interested in my response to our kids.

"I told myself I wasn't ticklish anymore, and then I wasn't."

"Can you turn it back on?" our daughter asked, wide-eyed.

"Nope, you can turn it off but not back on."

My kids laughed, but I know they were intrigued. I still get asked on a weekly basis if I can try to turn it on again. Not happening.

I tell this story for multiple reasons. First and foremost, if you want to do something and you want it bad enough, tell yourself exactly what you want and go make it happen. Stop making excuses and pointing your finger. Stop blaming your parents for the DNA they passed down to you. Stop putting it off until next year or after your vacation. It's all upstairs, and you're in control.

It's all upstairs in your mind, and the switch is your mindset.

Ideas to Consider and Share

Do you have any mental tricks that help get you through training, a race, or tough times?

Share your stories on Instagram, Facebook, Twitter, and Strava.

 #RUNLAP

Chapter Forty-Three

THE BACKWARD AND FORWARD RACE

When an idea becomes reality, that's something special.

Welcome to December. I'd run eleven marathons this year and was staring in the face of my toughest race yet.

I started adding up all the marathons I'd ever run and realized December's would be number nineteen. Being someone who likes even numbers and loves a challenge, I decided to add an additional marathon to finish 2017 with an even twenty. I could have chosen another race, and I actually looked into other options but decided to try something new, different, and challenging. I would run this race backward in the middle of the night at 1:00 a.m. and then turn around to run the "real" marathon with everyone else. This was unchartered territory for me and the farthest I'd ever run.

Before we get to the race, here's a little backstory. In March, even before the double marathon was an idea, I reached out to my run crew from around the country with a question. "Want to come to California and run this final marathon of the year with me? What do you think?"

Initially there was lots of interest. "That's an awesome idea! Let me see what I can do."

And as the months passed, the group of seven dwindled down to one. I know many of my friends wanted to join me, but family and other work logistics made it impossible. The runner with me for the second marathon would be my very good friend, Jessica Cabeen. I call her a good friend now, but when she officially committed, we still hadn't met in person. Remember what I said about your virtual crew? It's important to have those people all around the country. Jessica and I finally met during one of my speaking trips to Minnesota, and she made plans to run with me in Sacramento, California, on December 3, 2017.

At the time, and by her own admission, Jessica wasn't a marathon runner. She ran a marathon fifteen years prior but nothing since. She wasn't even a consistent runner, but she was determined to train, and train she did. She put her heart and soul into this race, and we would need each other for those final few miles in December.

When I told my wife about this double marathon plan, she had only one request.

"Adam (She never calls me Adam.), I want someone to run with you during the middle of the night."

That's all she needed to say, and I knew just the person to call. We have many great neighbors and friends I could have asked, but no one would be as excited as Andreas. We were hanging out at the pool one afternoon, and I popped the question.

"Hey, man, you know I'm running a bunch of marathons this year."

"Yeah, for sure. How's it all going?" he asked.

"Really awesome. I'm planning to run my December marathon twice."

"What do you mean . . . twice?"

Andreas is a beast. He's done Ironmans. He's done RAM (Race Across America), where he rode his bike across the country. He's a legit skier. And he has three young kids, so the energy level and stoke factor is always high.

"I'm going to run the course backward in the middle of the night at 1:00 a.m. and then run the real race. Do you want to do it with me?"

"Done!"

I had my security entourage, which would come in handy.

This is what the three weeks after the New York Marathon looked like leading up to this race. I worked every day. I ran 30- and 35-mile training runs on the weekends. Made final arrangements with Jessica for her trip to California. Considered all possible logistics with food, clothing, weather, gear, hydration, hotel accommodations, my family, and a whole host of other elements.

Two days before the race, Jessica and her son were flying in and landing around 11:00 p.m. I was also meeting with a videographer who was making a video about my marathon year. Friday night I had to meet with him and record some footage then zoom to the San Francisco airport to pick up Jessica. I got to bed that night around midnight and was up at 5:00 a.m. the next day to meet with the videographer and get some footage around my hometown. This was the day before I was running 52.4 miles.

After filming we got home around 10:00 a.m., packed up our gear, and drove the hour to Sacramento, so we could get our bibs and swag from the expo. It was Jessica's first time in Sacramento, so we toured the state capital, walked around, and grabbed some dinner. At 5:00 p.m. my neighbor (and another friend) were still at home. We still had to drive his car to the starting line, so he could get home after our middle of the night run, which was happening in just a few hours.

They got stuck in traffic and didn't get to the hotel until 9:00. Thankfully, someone in my crew (my wife) followed them to the starting point and drove them back to the hotel for a couple of hours of sleep.

The "real" marathon started at 7:00 a.m. the next day, and I wanted to leave plenty of time for my first run—just in case we hit a snag during the night. Leaving at 1:00 a.m. from the finish line would give me more than enough time to run, change my clothes at the start, get something to eat, and cue up with all the other runners. Andreas and our other neighbor Roux, were going to ride their bikes with me. They had a kid-trailer full of supplies—and some "protection" in case anything came up. As we left the hotel parking lot and headed to the finish line (my start line), I noticed a baseball bat in Andreas' trailer.

"Is that a baseball bat, bro?"

"Heck, yeah! You never know what might happen!"

Thankfully we didn't need it.

We started across the "finish" line at exactly 1:00 a.m. Within a few steps, a feeling came over my body that I've never had before—a mix of elation, uncertainty, and excitement. This was a big deal. It was the culmination of a big year and a celebration of sorts.

I ran, and my friends rode. We chatted. We checked the map. It started to rain. We had to ask for directions. We laughed. We stopped for a minute to eat. We laughed some more. They rode ahead to scout out the route. They took pictures. I posted on social media. And we checked the map some more.

I felt super strong and was on pace to run a 4:00 marathon. Jessica was meeting me at the start of the second marathon, and we vowed to run together for that entire race. So I did what I knew how to do; I ran. I ran with how my body felt, with how my friends were feeling and helping me along. And before we knew it, there they were. The buses. Lines and lines of school buses bringing the runners to the start.

The California International Marathon starts at Lake Folsom and finishes at the state capitol building in Sacramento. This was my fifth time running this race, and the emotions were pretty high as we finished those last two miles. I couldn't see the finish, but I could feel it.

The buses were stuck in a line, and we could feel all the runners looking at us. Were they wondering why we were running to the start? Did any of them fathom what we'd done? It didn't matter. This was our race and our experience. I almost started to cry. We crossed the start line in 4:04 and celebrated with a photo and hugs all around.

Thankfully, Andreas' car hadn't been towed during the middle of the night. I needed to change into some dry clothes, eat, and find my running partner for the second half. I hopped in the car, stripped off my wet clothes, put on some dry ones, ate, went to the bathroom, ate some more, found Jessica, and joined the thousands of other runners.

Once again, I felt something I'd never felt before. Looking around the crowd of runners, there were so many thoughts in my brain. I'd just run 26.2 miles and was about to run it again. Nobody else here had done that. I didn't feel superior to the other racers; I felt superior to the person I was one year ago. When you live a reality you'd only dreamed about, that's something special.

But we had work to do. Jessica was with me, and we were ready to roll.

Before the race and throughout our training, we talked about a time goal. I was predicting we'd be somewhere between 4:30 and 4:45, but it was really hard to estimate. The first thirteen miles were a breeze. We talked. We ate. We looked around, and we talked some more. This was the longest period of time we'd ever spent together, so we had lots to talk about. My wife and family were at Mile 15, and hearing those cowbells really lifted our spirits. My body felt strong and so was my mind, but I still had eleven miles to go and had already run forty-one. So I stayed calm and did a quick check-in with Stacy.

She knows the right questions to ask and what to look for.

Had I been hydrating?

Did I have enough to eat?

How were my legs feeling?

What was I thinking about?

After Stacy kissed me and told me I looked great, Jessica and I were back on the course, ready to crush the final eleven miles. These final miles were hard. Truly hard. We'd run a bit then walk for thirty seconds. Run again for another mile and walk for forty-five seconds. I could hear my friend's breathing and could tell her heart rate was beginning to climb, which isn't a great sign during a marathon. So we drank some fluids and power walked. And then I started talking.

I talked about all the people who have been such a big influence in my life. How they've helped to shape who I am. I talked about all the spectators who were cheering the runners—and thanked a few as we ran. I talked about the volunteers at the aid station, giving water and raking up all the discarded cups. And I talked about how thankful I was to have a friend who would fly across the country to run 26.2 miles with me and how a friendship like that is hard to come by in life. And we continued to run.

These are the moments. The moments that count but nobody sees. These aren't the moments that get posted on social media and shared with friends. These moments are for me. They are a quiet celebration of all the hard work that went in to get me to this point. Right here, right now. I don't need anyone to see those moments because most people probably wouldn't understand. These are the moments that count. This is my *why*.

We crossed that finish line in 4:48, and, *oh, my gosh*, it felt good. Was I tired? You bet I was. But any pain I felt was completely smothered by accomplishment. We linked up with our families and sat on the steps of the state capitol to recap the race.

Jessica and her son were flying home that night, and we needed to celebrate. After a quick tour of the Golden Gate Bridge, we had dinner at the Ferry Building in San Francisco and then said goodbye to our friends at the airport.

I fell asleep on the way home and woke up—not reflecting but thinking about what was next. This backward and forward marathon had been the most challenging endeavor of my life. There were a few moments to celebrate. But there was work to do. I took Monday off from running and cranked it back up Tuesday morning at 4:00. If I thought that race was a challenge, I had much more in store on New Year's Eve, only a few shorts weeks away.

Ideas to Consider and Share

What was it like accomplishing something that was completely new and different for you? How did it feel? What type of preparation went into it? What did you learn?

Share your stories on Instagram, Facebook, Twitter, and Strava.

 **#RUNLAP**

Chapter Forty-Four

NEW YEAR'S EVE

Twenty-four hours is a long time to run.

I never intended to run this race. Why would anyone running thirteen marathons in one year want to add one more to the calendar? It happened the way most things happen: by chance.

In June of 2017, I was looking at the race website for my night marathon and somehow stumbled onto their *entire* calendar. I was not looking for another race, but there it was: "New Year's Eve One Day." I remember trying to wrap my head around the concept of running for twenty-four hours straight. I quickly skipped to my race calendar and realized my December marathon (the backward and forward race) was happening early in the month. *I would have time to recover!* And the double marathon would actually be great training for a twenty-four-hour race. *What am I going to tell my wife?*

So I didn't. I put it on my race calendar but didn't sign up. I was now officially (in my brain) going to run this thing. But if I signed up now, my wife would see the credit card transaction and have questions—not money questions but sanity questions. I needed to find my point of entry to drop it into a conversation. I'd find the right time and was pumped for a new adventure.

I did a Google search for, "How to train for a 24-hour race" and devoured articles written by runners who partook in such events and were kind enough to blog about their experience. Some of these races happen on a track, some on a three-mile loop, and mine was taking place at Crissy Field in San Francisco at the base of the Golden Gate Bridge around a one-mile loop. I've been there many times, and it really is a special place.

What a perfect way to finish my marathon year! This would be the icing on the double marathon cake.

I read an article written by a guy on the east coast who decided to run the twenty-four-hour race but hadn't trained much. He went out too fast and "only" ran for eighteen hours. He ended up running seventy miles but could hardly walk after the race. I felt confident because I was training. *Not a problem*, I told myself, and I set a goal.

One hundred miles. My goal was to run one hundred miles in that race—almost doubling the longest I'd ever run before. This was the suffering, the pain, the challenge, and the journey I wanted.

I finally found the right time to tell my wife about this race. We were in the middle of our favorite ten mile loop, our kids were riding their bikes with us, and I just came clean and told her. "You know this year so far has been awesome with all my marathons. I've learned so much about myself, and I want to really finish the year off strong. There's this twenty-four hour race on New Year's Eve I'm going to do, and my mom already said she'd watch the kids!"

"Okay, sounds good."

Well, that was easy!

[Telling Stacy]

Fast forward from June to New Year's Eve—the final day of my marathon year.

I made meticulous notes and packed everything I'd need in order to run nonstop for twenty-four hours—and probably many things I wouldn't need, but contingency planning for an event like this is important. Some friends offered to run a few miles with me, but I actually wanted to be alone. I wanted to fight off the demons by myself that day.

I began to realize that all the marathons were just a precursor to this race. I was more excited than ever but didn't know what to expect.

The race website had some information but not much detail. I'd looked at results from previous years, but most people ran the six or twelve hour option. The race started at 9:00 a.m. on New Year's Eve and finished at 9:00 a.m. on New Year's Day.

We pulled up to the parking lot, and a number of tents were set up. Then I remembered all the references to tents I'd read about in my research. Like an all-night race, it finally dawned on me. Some people bring tents, so they can take a break and nap if they need to. I brought an old camp chair but had no intention of taking a nap.

Ten minutes before 9:00 a.m., the race director called everyone over to review the instructions. We all wore a transponder around our ankles that would count laps. The race started in a counter-clockwise direction, but we were free to change directions throughout the day if we wanted. "Good luck," he told us, "and have fun," and we were off.

I was hoping to run nine-minute miles for as long as I could. That was a comfortable pace for me, though I knew it wouldn't last forever. But if I could get some serious mileage at that pace, I could deal with the overnight miles and whatever I needed to do early in the morning to achieve my goal.

I don't listen to music when I run and never have. For most of my marathons, I carried my phone during the race but then decided I didn't want the extra weight on my arm. I even bought a lighter water bottle for this race, so I could conserve as much energy as possible.

Since the course was a one-mile loop, food and gear was in easy reach at any point throughout the day. The organizers also had great snacks for everyone and even some nice surprises late in the race.

I ran. Some people stopped. I ran. More people stopped. I continued to run. And some people took a nap.

The six-hour people came and went like I was running in a time-lapse video. I saw some people for hours and hours, and then they disappeared. Some people looked solid and strong on the course, until they stopped to barf. Others started breathing heavily, which is never a good sign, and then they were passed out in a chair.

At midnight, the twelve-hour crew had come and gone. It was just the twenty-four hour runners—about fifteen or twenty of us. The fireworks went off by the Bay Bridge, the race director opened champagne for the twelve-hour finishers, there was pizza, and I continued to run.

But I wasn't alone. I'm not talking about the other runners or spectators. I started thinking about my dad.

I'm not religious, and I don't believe in a higher power, but I know my dad was there with me during those long, dark miles. He was encouraging me—telling me I could do it. Because I know if he was still alive, he would have camped out at that race with me for the entire day. He'd have been so proud of what I had already accomplished and what I was trying to accomplish. And he would be telling all of his friends about it. Cancer had a different agenda for my dad, but I know he was around. And I kept running.

In my pre-race research, I wondered if it would happen to me. *Would I see things on the course?*

I've read many books and articles where runners talk about seeing or hearing things on the trail in the middle of the night. A tree stump is a person, gummy bears dancing under the trees, voices calling out as they ran. Each lap I would find some landmark and tell myself what it was, and I was never wrong. No hallucinations. So I kept on running.

I taught elementary school for years, but math isn't my strongest subject. In the middle of the night, after running ninety miles, the calculations were going to be tough. I counted down the miles, looked at my watch, forgot how many miles, and repeated my labored computations. I really wanted to run a hundred miles, my pace was still strong, and I had only walked a few miles up until this point.

At 3:00 a.m., I'd run ninety miles and only had ten more to go. I could do this math: I had six hours to run ten miles.

Any day of the week, even the day after a marathon, running ten miles would only take me about ninety minutes on an average training day. This wasn't any average day, and my body knew it.

During the New York Marathon, I ran a few miles with Dean Karnazes, and he'd said this race was on his calendar. I was excited to see Dean in action at this race and had the honor of running a few laps with him. I wouldn't say he was freaked out, but I remember his comment. He was trying to qualify for the Spartan race in Greece, which is 152 miles across the country. He originally thought he had to run 108 miles to automatically qualify but just found out it was 112 miles. He had his game face on. Four extra miles were four extra miles. We chatted, I stopped for some lentil soup, and he continued on.

I was still running, but my pace had definitely slowed. I took more walk breaks on each lap and continued to think about my dad. He kept me going. He was chirping in my ear that we would celebrate later. He continued to tell me how proud he was. And I continued to run.

Twenty-four hours, to state the obvious, is a long time to run. My best advice to anyone is to just find a groove and stay in it as long as you can. Find a song you can sing to yourself and sing it as long as you can. Find some people to run with and run with them as long as you can. Just make sure you run your race and don't let anyone derail your plan. Find parts of the course that you like and smile whenever you go by. Find parts of the course that you don't like and look away every time you go past. Find food that is appealing and eat a lot of it. Find something to drink that you like and drink a lot of it. Find your groove and stay in that groove.

There's a line, and you need to cross it. Then draw a new line, and cross it. Repeat. That's a twenty-four-hour race.

At 6:00 a.m., I crossed the ninety-five-mile mark and knew I was home free. I had three hours to run five miles and knew I was going to complete my goal.

I started to cry.

Over the years, my daughter has asked me why I never cry, and I didn't have a good answer. I cried when my kids were born, when Stacy and I got married, and when my mother-in-law and dad passed away from long battles with cancer. Other than that, I don't cry. Until now.

The emotions from running thirteen marathons overtook me. The pain that I ignored finally overtook me. And the pain I knew my dad went through with round after round of chemotherapy and in those final days before he passed—all of it overtook me. And then I saw my wife.

Stacy had worked the day before until 9:00 p.m., and I know they were busy at the hospital. She planned to meet me in the morning and drive me home. I'd been checking my phone off and on, but at this point, I was in full focus mode and didn't know when she would arrive. As I ran my ninety-fifth lap and turned the corner on the backstretch, there she was. And I was crying.

She brought along our dog, Bear, and I gave them both a huge hug. Surprised by my tears, she thought I was hurt. But I told her this was an intensely emotional experience, and I was letting it flow. She started to cry too. We ran, and we walked. I told her about the night miles and how I felt. At the start, I counted at least fifteen tents and hundreds of chairs. Now we were down to only about twenty chairs.

I told her about the fireworks at midnight to bring in the New Year. I told her about the homeless person sleeping on the bench all night and how I'd passed him time and time again and wished there was something I could do to help him. I told her about the people we saw yesterday morning at Crissy Field, who were now back again walking their dogs. And we were still running. I told her what I'd eaten, how much I drank, about all the bowls of lentil soup that tasted so good, and that I was tired… but strangely, feeling strong.

And then I crossed the line. One-hundred miles in twenty-three hours. I confirmed my transponder with the race director and turned to my wife. She gave me a big hug and asked me a question.

"You're not stopping, are you?"

It was now 8:00 a.m., and I'd been running for twenty-three straight hours. I had achieved my goal of running 100 miles. But this wasn't a 100-mile race. It was a twenty-four-hour race, and I had an hour to go.

The question now was how many more miles could I run in one hour? That turned into my challenge, and I continued to suffer. I'll admit that something in my brain clicked off after passing 100 and that final hour was tough. Really tough. My upper body still felt strong, but everything down below was in hurt-mode. I could feel blisters on my feet but didn't bother to look at them hours before when I changed socks. My quads and calves were tired and begging me to stop. My brain had a different agenda. My mind was still functional, and I quizzed myself on multiplication tables, names of family members and their birth dates, the make and model of my car, and I passed with flying colors. I think.

At 9:00 a.m. on New Year's Day 2017, I crossed the line after running 103 miles.

My body was thrashed. Little by little, over twenty-four hours, I made requests of it that had never been made before. I tapped into my internal bandwidth and utilized all those training miles for this final test. But I couldn't bend over to take the transponder off of my ankle, and thankfully, a race volunteer was there to help. My body was done, and my brain was as well.

I hobbled over to my trusty old camp chair and downed a few chocolate almond milks and some bananas. I had to eat but wasn't hungry. My wife helped me change into clean and dry clothes, and we got ready for the award ceremony.

When you run a race, they give you a medal. When you run 100 miles, they give you a belt buckle. I was about to get my buckle. Only five runners ran 100 miles; I was one of them. There have only been a few times since my dad passed away where I really wished he was there; this was one of those times.

I got my buckle, we hopped in the car, and I immediately fell asleep.

Some people encouraged me to write this chapter the day after the race. I didn't. The memories of that day have been so intently imprinted on my brain, I knew there wouldn't be a detail that would escape me. When you take on a challenge like running for twenty-four hours, it's not something you can easily forget. The smells, the sights, the pain, the people, and the buckle—they stay with you forever. Trust me.

I took two full weeks off from any type of running after this race and got back into it slowly. Soon after the twenty-four-hour race, I learned I'd be running the Boston Marathon the following April. One of the race sponsors was putting together a team of educators, and I'd been chosen from an application pool of over 1,600 people.

Ideas to Consider and Share

When did you have to dig really deep to accomplish something? How did it make you feel?

Share your stories on Instagram, Facebook, Twitter, and Strava.

#RUNLAP

Chapter Forty-Five

DREAMS

Have a dream. Come up with a plan.
And go make it happen.

*D*reams are different than goals. We all have dreams, but few have goals. Running thirteen marathons and a twenty-four-hour race in one year was a goal.

My dream is to run across the United States. I may never have the time, I may never find the tenacity to attempt it, but it's still a dream.

People sometimes talk about dreams like they're farfetched and could never happen. But dreams can become real.

Maybe you need to start by setting small goals and enjoying some success to feed your imagination. But keep your dreams close by. None of us know what tomorrow looks like, so we must chase after our dreams today.

#RunLAP Reflections from Ryan Sheehy
Principal, California, @sheehyrw

I joined the cross-country team in college, where I struggled to keep up daily in the miles. The competition was out of my league, but I continued to show up. I competed in races, learned humility, and was part of a team. The experience left me knowing that I didn't necessarily love running, but I fell in love with the feeling that running gave me.

Years later, I am still running and love a good challenge. In January 2017, Adam Welcome challenged me to run a marathon with him in December. I handled this like most challenges; I jumped in with both feet without thinking about it too much.

I researched plans, nutrition, and gear. I was ready to start running more miles with a goal in mind. For the next few months, I created a base. In July the official training began, and I was on the plan without missing a beat. In the first few months, I hit ten miles with ease, which shocked me. The base and build up were working. I kept telling myself that I could do this—I would complete this marathon!

Unfortunately, life had other plans. In September, while at home, I broke my ankle, which required surgery. After eight weeks in a wheelchair, my marathon hopes were gone, but the spirit was still alive. I wouldn't be running a marathon in 2017, but I was alive and could walk.

This experience taught me that everyone has a marathon ahead of them. They all look different, but all need training nonetheless. You will get knocked down, and it takes strength to get back up and keep moving forward. I am glad that this all happened because it has taught me lessons that I would not understand otherwise.

Ideas to Consider and Share

What are your dreams? And what are you going to do in order to make them happen?

Share your stories on Instagram,
Facebook, Twitter, and Strava.

#RUNLAP

WHATEVER YOU DO,
DO IT 100%—LIFE IS
TOO DANG SHORT TO BE
MEDIOCRE AND ONLY
GIVE 60%—GO MAKE
IT HADDEN!

Chapter Forty-Six

Pain

C'mon! So many people have it far worse.

*Y*our brain is in charge. It really is. It controls your pain and stamina threshold. It dictates your situation and determines whether you'll continue or quit. Pain doesn't last forever, and I constantly tell myself that during a race. At least that's what I believe.

I hadn't thought about pain, deeply anyway, until I ran for twenty-four hours on New Year's Eve. Going in, I knew I'd experience some level of pain as I moved my body towards the goal of 100 miles. I'd approach pain like I approached being ticklish. If I told myself I wasn't in pain—that I was okay and could keep going—then I could do it.

But something happened in the middle of the night during that race. I hadn't planned for it. Nobody warned me to be on the look-out, but it floated to the surface of my brain—and was quite possibly the biggest gift of all from my marathon year. And it has to do with my dad.

Late at night, after running for many hours and upwards of eighty miles, I had a realization. I'd been with my dad since that first appointment when the doctor told him he had cancer. I took many days off from work over the years, going to appointments with him, evaluating the latest diagnosis and what the next steps would entail. And I was with him the day he took his last breath, when he still wanted to fight but cancer outflanked him and his doctors. I held his hand as they pronounced that he was gone, and all I could think about was the pain. He wouldn't have to deal with any more rounds of chemo—no more trials that might give him a few extra months to live. No more "chemo-brain" that made my dad do odd things and act in a way that wasn't really him. That was over.

Very late that night, I made a promise to myself. I would never again complain about pain.

There was absolutely nothing I could voluntarily put myself through that would be anywhere close to the pain my dad dealt with for five long years. I chose to run all those races. I chose to train in the dark, cold, and rain. I was getting exactly what I asked for. He didn't ask to get cancer and have it take his life, and there was no way my marathon year was going to cause me any type of pain. In some weird way, I felt like I was running for my dad. He wasn't a runner, not even close, but I was digesting my own pain to somehow put me closer to all that he went through. His sickness showed me what it was like to live, to go after things that seemed just a bit out of reach, and to not stop until it was over.

There's not a moment that goes by where I don't think about him. I'm sure all people have that feeling about loved ones they've lost. But my dad was extra special. I learned so much from him, but the biggest lesson of all is one he doesn't he even know about. Throughout those twenty-four hours, he reminded me to kick pain in the face and keep on going, to not let circumstances define you, to not give people the ability to judge you or tell you what you're capable of, and to not listen to the pain—even when it won't go away.

The pain will be there when you're done, and we can deal with it then. I'm busy living my life and getting after it. How about you?

Ideas to Consider and Share

Put yourself in a situation with a high probability you're going to have some pain, and challenge yourself. Prepare your mind before you start and push the pain aside as you go.

Share your stories on Instagram, Facebook, Twitter, and Strava.

WE OFTEN PUT ARBITRARY
LIMITS ON OURSELVES
WITHOUT EVEN TAKING
THE FIRST STEP.

Chapter Forty-Seven

THE HARDEST PART

Do what you need to do,
and you'll be good.

After 2017 was over, there was one question people asked more than any other.

"What was the hardest part?"

The question itself gives some clues into what people are most interested in. Very few people asked me which race was my favorite. Or what it was like running all those races on a vegan diet. Hardly anyone even asked if I would do it again. Two people asked me what I eat during a marathon, let alone while running for twenty-four straight hours. Nobody really cared what type of shoes I wore, how many pairs I went through in 2017, or how many miles I ran that year with races and training combined.

The vast majority of people wanted to know what the hardest part was. And they were a bit disappointed with my answer.

I always paused for a minute before responding, to bring the proper amount of gravity to my reply.

"It wasn't that hard." Then another pause. "It really wasn't."

People always gave an awkward look as they awaited further explanation.

Were there moments of struggle and pain? You bet. But the entire year wasn't hard. From the very beginning, I was committed to my goal—and energized by my goal. I made plans to train. I took my dialed-in diet and made it even better. I invested in a coach halfway through the year to make sure I'd be ready for those big days in December. I have a strong family who supported me all 365 days as I focused on what I needed to do. I didn't leave anything to chance.

People say they're going to do something but don't put the pieces in place to achieve their goals. They don't properly train. Halfway through they get sidetracked, and their goals go by the wayside. It gets too hard, and they give up. They haven't told enough friends, and they're missing the social pressure that's so important to achieve big things. When you have that approach, when you sabotage your own dream, then it really is hard.

I told myself what I wanted to do. I told myself I was going to. And I made plans to do it.

I had thoughts of getting injured during training. It didn't happen. I had slight apprehension about eating only plants for an entire year and asking a lot of my body in return. Plants have more than enough fuel, and my performance was spot on. I'd done my homework about a vegan diet and didn't just try it on a whim; it was a calculated decision. A few races only gave me a week in between them, and I wasn't sure if I'd have enough recovery time to run a solid race. I did fine—and some of those races were my best. Prepare your body and mind and it will come through for you in the clutch.

You can go into something ill-prepared and maybe you'll be successful. I'd rather prepare, so I'm ready when the time comes. That's the hardest part about accomplishing big things.

Ideas to Consider and Share

Think about something you've tried and failed at in the past. What would you have done differently to ensure success the next time around?

> Share your stories on Instagram,
> Facebook, Twitter, and Strava.
>

ANYTHING YOU REALLY WANT TO DO IN LIFE IS GOING TO BE HARD.

Chapter Forty-Eight

My Favorite Smoothie

Smoothies are so good, even when your
friends make a face at you.

I've been blending smoothies for years. My family loves them, and
they're a great way to start the day.

This recipe is my foundation and allows for plenty of variety. I
don't always measure everything perfectly, which drives my wife nuts.
Experiment and see what you like most.

2 cups of liquid (I vary between water, coconut water, almond
milk, and usually have a combination of at least two.)

2 cups (or handfuls) of spinach or kale

1/2 beet (If you don't have a beet, just leave it out.)

2 stalks of celery

1 or 1-1/2 frozen bananas

1 cup of frozen blueberries

2 tablespoons peanut or almond butter (Sometimes I use coconut butter instead.)

5-6 dates (Make sure you take out the pit.)

1 tablespoon chia seeds

1 teaspoon spirulina (Sometimes)

Sometimes I'll leave out the spirulina or celery. I always include the liquids, spinach or kale, bananas, blueberries, peanut/almond/coconut butter, chia seeds, and the dates. If you don't have dates, that's fine; it just makes the smoothie a little bit sweeter, which I like. Also note that this makes a pretty big smoothie. You can put in a little bit less of each ingredient to make less. If I'm in a hurry or not that hungry, I'll just blend water, spinach, celery, bananas, and chia seeds, and it's still really good and fills me up.

Sometimes I don't include beets if I've had them three days in a row. (If you use beets, don't forget; and if you've used beets before, you know what I'm talking about!)" To prepare the beets, take all the skin off, cut it up into smaller pieces, put in a pot, and cover the beets with water. Boil for twelve to fifteen minutes and wash them off. They keep in the refrigerator for days if you want to prepare ahead of time.

If you want a chunkier smoothie and enjoy dates, blend everything together *except* the dates, then drop them in and blend for another fifteen seconds. This will leave the dates in small chunks, which is a nice surprise when you drink it up.

Happy blending, and please share your favorite recipes using the #RunLAP hashtag!

Chapter Forty-Nine

RUNNING TIPS FROM ADAM AND FRIENDS

We are always training.

- You only get one body. Take care of it.
- What you eat is up to you. Develop discipline and it won't be difficult.
- Finding time to stretch is hard. But if you do, you'll feel better.
- If it's raining, I'm training, because when it's not, I'll appreciate the weather even more.
- When it's extremely hot, be careful. Your body can get depleted quickly in the heat, and it takes time to recover.
- Don't wear your running shoes for too many months. Your body will tell you when it's time for a new pair.
- Vary your training. Don't always run at the same time or along the same routes. Shake it up and keep things fresh.
- Focus on the big picture rather than the endless details of equipment. If you have shoes, you can run. The little stuff is just little stuff and can weigh you down.
- If you're stuck in a rut, take some time off, hire a coach, cross train, watch some races on YouTube, follow some runners on social media, run shorter (or longer), run earlier (or later). And see if you can smile and run at the same time.

Invest in a good pair of running shoes.
—Kati Mann, Ohio

Set your alarm and go before the
day hijacks your plan.
—Dave Schmittou, Florida

Start in small steps. Don't overdo at first, but do!
—Greg Fairchild, Illinois

Be patient with yourself and find a crew that
shares similar goals. They will push you.
—Andrea Kornowski, Wisconsin

CONCLUSION

’m not an Olympian. I didn't receive a college scholarship to play
sports. I'm just a guy who decided I wasn't going to stand on
the sidelines and wonder, *What if.* I'm not going to let this precious
opportunity called life pass me by without putting myself out there
and seeing what I'm made of.

And let me tell you, it's not too late for any of us. If you're under
the age of ninety-nine, you still have time. Don't let any type of regret
crawl into your soul. There are plenty of races left to run, but you
probably won't receive a personal invitation from the organizers. So
please allow me to invite you.

Yes, it's going to take work and dedication. But please do accept
the challenge. People complain about not winning the lottery—and
never even buy a ticket.

I believe in you.

I know that you can.

I trust in your abilities.

I've seen it done by so many before you.

I know it's going to be hard.

But it's so worth it!

Go out and get yours; it's time.

Peace!

~Adam

Epilogue: Boston

Wednesday, December 6, 2017, was the day my dream of running the 2018 Boston Marathon became more than just an idea. My legs were feeling strong, even though it was only three days since I'd run the double marathon, and in three short weeks, I'd had the biggest run of my life with the twenty-four-hour run on New Year's Eve.

I'd taken off two full days with no running at all, and it was my first day back with a short four-mile run and then a full day of work. My boss texted me that morning saying we needed to meet later in the day at his office. The tone of the message was super weird. We have an amazing working relationship and were actually principals together in a different district, and simply put, we know each other really well and get along great. When I dug deeper, he replied, "We just need to meet." It was weird, and I knew something was up. I also knew (at least I thought I knew) that if something was wrong or I was in trouble at work, he would tell me ahead of time. I wasn't too worried, but there was still something about the meeting I couldn't put my finger on.

The day went by, and at 2:30, we met in his office. Our conversation started by us chatting together about some other work-related things, and then his phone rang. It was a FaceTime call and not a regular phone call; I could tell by how the ring sounded. He was chatting with someone who I didn't know and then turned his phone on me. There was a guy who I didn't know staring at me, then he asked me a question.

The guy: "Did you run this morning?"

Me: "Of course, I did. Did you?"

The guy: "No, I didn't, but you're running the Boston Marathon in April."

I turned around, and there was a huge crowd of people in our district office cheering, laughing, and smiling. And then it all made sense.

A few months ago, someone had sent me a link for a contest that a company (Hylands) who is a sponsor for the Boston Marathon was putting on. They were putting together a team of educators from across the country to run the Boston Marathon in April. I clicked on the link, submitted my application, and actually had two separate phone interviews with a couple of different people about the application. To be completely honest, I had kind of forgotten about the whole thing. I had just run a double marathon a few days prior, and my mind had been on other things!

But out of more than 1,600 applicants, they chose seventeen educators from across the country, and I was on the team! They'd called my district office to set up the surprise call, and what a surprise it was!

My wife has been talking about Boston our entire relationship, as she'd qualified and run it a few years before we met. For me to qualify in my age bracket, though, I had to run a 3:08 marathon, and I've never run anywhere near that fast. This was my ticket, and off I went to Boston. You can bet I was super excited.

It was, of course, pretty special being in Boston. But the energy of this team of educators made it even more special. We all instantly had a bond, had things to talk about (other than running), and were all equally amped for this race. Until we looked at the weather forecast. It was bad, really bad, and it turned out to be the worst weather in thirty-five years for the race.

One thing I always remind myself is to trust in your training, don't overthink things, and do what you would normally do for any other race. Don't change your game plan at the last minute, even if the temperature is in the low thirties and you have a thirty-mile-an-hour headwind and torrential rain the entire race. Even then, do your thing.

That's exactly what we had, and that's what I did.

I've run in some pretty bad weather through the years, but the weather in 2018 for the Boston Marathon was some of the worst combined conditions I've ever been in. The temperature was in the low thirties with a "real feel" in the high twenties. The headwind was no joke and stayed between twenty-five and thirty miles an hour for the entire race. And the rain. I train in the rain all the time, but California rain is different from New England rain, and it was cold.

Let me tell you something about this race. It was nasty, the conditions were horrible, it was like running through a huge puddle in the pouring rain with a crazy headwind and the temps were cold for the entire 26.2 miles, but it was still just a race. People around me were doing things that they normally would never do when running a marathon. In that kind of weather, you're going to get wet and be wet, no matter what; there's just no avoiding it.

Trust in your training. Do what you normally do. Throw on an extra, lightweight jacket to help keep you warm. And just go run.

I'll say it again: This is why you should push yourself in training. It's why you should run when you're tired. When you're hungry. When it's raining. In the middle of the night. With not enough layers. In uncomfortable conditions. That way, when you're in the worst of conditions on race day in the most prestigious marathon in the world, it's not that big of a deal.

Don't think it wasn't a hard race for me; every marathon is tough. But everything that was happening with the weather wasn't that big of a deal. My approach was to focus on what I could control, enjoy the energy of Boston, stay positive, eat and drink, and tell Mother Nature that she wasn't going to beat me that day.

I ran. And I ran strong. I felt the weather, but I didn't think about it. I focused on my body. My breathing. My fluids. My pace. What I was eating. I seriously just blocked out the weather and ran a super-solid 3:43 and couldn't have been happier with my race. A record number of people dropped out of the race or didn't even start, and many got hypothermia. There were reports of medical aid stations on the course getting so full they had to open a church nearby for all the overflow runners.

The Boston Marathon of 2018 will be one to remember. For me, it was one more affirmation to continue the work I've always done. Do hard things. Be consistent. Eat good food. Push myself more than I'm comfortable with. Smile. Surround myself with others who feel the same way. And never *ever* think or say that I can't. Because if you want it bad enough, you can do whatever you want.

Acknowledgments

I have many people to thank and acknowledge. My parents for always encouraging me to work harder and strive to be more and do more. You've shown me what's possible in life, and I only hope I can do the same for my own children.

My wife, Stacy, for being my running partner and so much more in life on a daily basis. For supporting my ideas and antics and being the glue that holds our family together. My two children, Greta and Tilden, for supporting me and riding their bikes next to us as we run every weekend to get our miles in and always ringing those cowbells when I see them on the marathon course.

To my running coach in 2017, Sally McRae, who is an absolutely amazing runner, mentor, and advocate, and whom I learned so much from and owe so much of my running success to.

To my speaking agent, Ryan Giffen, for encouraging me to write this book in the first place and for always being a stand-up human being in so many ways.

And finally, to all those people who run marathons. You don't know it, but I gain wisdom and inspiration from you. Running may seem like an individual sport, but in my eyes, it's very much about the team.

MORE FROM

DAVE BURGESS
Consulting, Inc.

Since 2012, DBCI has been publishing books that inspire and equip educators to be their best. For more information on our DBCI titles or to purchase bulk orders for your school, district, or book study, visit **DaveBurgessConsulting.com/DBCBooks**.

More from the PIRATE Series

Teach Like a PIRATE by Dave Burgess

eXPlore Like a Pirate by Michael Matera

Learn Like a Pirate by Paul Solarz

Play Like a Pirate by Quinn Rollins

Lead Like a PIRATE Series

Lead Like a PIRATE by Shelley Burgess and Beth Houf

Lead with Culture by Jay Billy

Lead with Literacy by Mandy Ellis

Balance Like a Pirate
by Jessica Cabeen, Jessica Johnson, and Sarah Johnson

Leadership & School Culture

Culturize by Jimmy Casas

Escaping the School Leader's Dunk Tank
by Rebecca Coda and Rick Jetter

The Innovator's Mindset by George Couros

Kids Deserve It! by Todd Nesloney and Adam Welcome

Let Them Speak by Rebecca Coda and Rick Jetter

The Limitless School by Abe Hege and Adam Dovico

The Pepper Effect by Sean Gaillard

The Principled Principal
by Jeffrey Zoul and Anthony McConnell

The Secret Solution
by Todd Whitaker, Sam Miller, and Ryan Donlan

Start Right Now
by Todd Whitaker, Jeffrey Zoul, and Jimmy Casas

Unmapped Potential by Julie Hasson and Missy Lennard

Your School Rocks by Ryan McLane and Eric Lowe

Technology & Tools

50 Things You can Do with Google Classroom
by Alice Keeler and Libbi Miller

50 Things to Go Further with Google Classroom
by Alice Keeler and Libbi Miller

140 Twitter Tips for Educators
by Brad Currie, Billy Krakower, and Scott Rocco

Code Breaker by Brian Aspinall

Google Apps for Littles by Christine Pinto and Alice Keeler

Master the Media by Julie Smith

Shake Up Learning by Kasey Bell

Social LEADia by Jennifer Casa-Todd

Teaching Math with Google Apps
by Alice Keeler and Diana Herrington

Teaching Methods & Materials

All 4s and 5s by Andrew Sharos

Ditch That Homework by Matt Miller and Alice Keeler

Ditch That Textbook by Matt Miller

The EduProtocol Field Guide
by Marlena Hebern and Jon Corippo

Instant Relevance by Denis Sheeran

LAUNCH by John Spencer and A.J. Juliani

Pure Genius by Don Wettrick

Shift This! by Joy Kirr

Spark Learning by Ramsey Musallam

Sparks in the Dark by Travis Crowder and Todd Nesloney

Table Talk Math by John Stevens

The Classroom Chef by John Stevens and Matt Vaudrey

The Wild Card by Hope and Wade King

The Writing on the Classroom Wall by Steve Wyborney

Inspiration, Professional Growth & Personal Development

4 O'Clock Faculty by Rich Czyz

Be REAL by Tara Martin

Be the One for Kids by Ryan Sheehy

The EduNinja Mindset by Jennifer Burdis

How Much Water do We Have? by Pete and Kris Nunweiler

P Is for Pirate by Dave and Shelley Burgess

The Path to Serendipity by Allyson Aspey

Shattering the Perfect Teacher Myth by Aaron Hogan

Stories from Webb by Todd Nesloney

Talk to Me by Kim Bearden

The Zen Teacher by Dan Tricarico

About the Author

Adam Welcome has been a runner and athlete his entire life. In third grade, he had a teacher who pushed him farther than he thought was possible, and he broke six minutes for the mile run. That's when Adam realized he had more in his body and mind, and that has been with him ever since.

Adam is also an educator and has been a teacher, vice principal, principal, and director of innovation and technology. He also travels around the country to speak and work with school districts and other organizations throughout the year.

Adam was nominated for Technology Leader of the Year by *Tech & Learning* magazine in 2010, was recognized as Principal of the Year in 2013, winner of the East Bay CUE Site Leader of the Year in 2016, and most recently was selected by the National School Board Association as a "20 to Watch" in the nation.

In his spare time, Adam runs almost every day at 4:00 a.m., skis at Lake Tahoe with his family, hikes, travels, absolutely loves to run marathons, and has done twenty-two at the time of publication.

Connect with Adam Welcome

  @mradamwelcome

 mradamwelcome.com

CPSIA information can be obtained
at www.ICGtesting.com
Printed in the USA
BVHW04s0539100718
521242BV00009B/21/P